The History of the Berkeley Poets Cooperative
1968–1991

A History of the Times

For Penny
love
Marlee

Hip Pocket Press Mission Statement

It is our belief that the arts are the embodiment of the soul of a culture, that the promotion of writers and artists is essential if our current culture, with its emphasis on television and provocative outcomes, is to have a chance to develop that inner voice and ear that express and listen to beauty. Toward that end, Hip Pocket Press will continue to search out and discover poets and writers whose voices can give us a clearer understanding of ourselves and of the culture that defines us.

Other Books from Hip Pocket Press

You Notice the Body: Gail Rudd Entrekin (poetry)
Terrain: Dan Bellm, Molly Fisk, Forrest Hamer (poetry)
A Common Ancestor: Marilee Richards (poetry)
Sierra Songs & Descants: Poetry & Prose of the Sierra
Truth Be Told: Tom Farber (epigrams)
Songs for a Teenage Nomad: Kim Culbertson (young adult fiction)
Yuba Flows: Kirsten Casey, Gary Cooke, Cheryl Dumesnil, Judy
    Halebsky, Iven Lourie & Scott Young (poetry)
The More Difficult Beauty: Molly Fisk (poetry)
Ex Vivo (Out of the Living Body): Kirsten Casey (poetry)
Even That Indigo: John Smith (poetry)

Web Publications

Canary, a Literary Journal of the Environmental Crisis:
www.hippocketpress.org/canary
Sisyphus, Essays on Language, Culture & the Arts:
www.hippocketpress.org/sisyphus

The History of the Berkeley Poets Cooperative

1968-1991

A History of the Times

Edited by Charles Entrekin

HPP
HIP POCKET PRESS

Orinda, CA
2013

Published by Hip Pocket Press
5 Del Mar Court
Orinda, CA 94563
www.hippocketpress.org

This edition was produced for on-demand distribution by
lightningsource.com for Hip Pocket Press.

Typesetting: Wordsworth of Marin (wordsworthofmarin.com)
Cover art: Unknown (see Acknowledgments: A Word about the Cover)
Cover design: LeeAnn Brook (brookdesign.com)
Photograph of author: Steve Haimowitz (Berkeley, CA)
Proofreading Assistance: Judy Crowe

Printed in the United States of America.

ISBN 0-917658-39-6
ISBN 13: 978-0-917658-39-6

Acknowledgments

A Word about the Cover

The painting hangs in my living room, a found object, from a closeout sale, from a failed furniture store, from a coffee house that failed to open (signs of the times). An air of sensuality floats above her lifted cup, with a suggestion of anticipated pleasure. She has elegant hands, face and the stature of a beautiful woman, poised upon a pillow. This piece represents, for me, the spirit of the Berkeley Poets Cooperative; her stylized beauty survived despite the challenges around her. Should the creator of this painting see this work, please contact hippocketpress.org and we will be honored to give credit for the creation.

Special Thanks

Because I am suffering vision loss, I want to especially thank my editorial assistants, whose help and intelligent input have made this book possible.

Catherine Anderson's awesome technical skills and genius-level critical abilities were immensely useful in getting this project off the ground. Thank you, Catherine.

Zara Raab's editorial skills and experience were an invaluable assist after Catherine departed for Korea. Thanks, Zara.

And Heidi Varian's editorial suggestions, amazing perseverance, and wide-ranging skill sets have been invaluable in bringing the book to completion. My thanks, Heidi.

Many thanks to Judy Crowe for her tireless proofreading on this project.

And, of course, to my wife Gail Rudd Entrekin for her tolerance, and her proofreading and design input, my love and appreciation.

In Memoriam

Jaimes Alsop, Karen Brodine, Elizabeth (Betsy) Gladstone Huebner Dubovsky, Quinton Duval, John Gardner, Stan Rice, Dorien Ross, Laura Schiff, Rona Spalten.

The Berkeley Poets Cooperative was a nonprofit organization that offered writers the opportunity to explore, develop and publish their works. Our primary goals were threefold – to bring to the Berkeley community a literary magazine of high quality, to maintain a free workshop open to all writers, and to publish outstanding collections of poetry and fiction by individual writers.

"The Berkeley Poets Cooperative publishes some of the most accomplished work I have thus far come across in my efforts to define what is being done… in Bay Area Poetry."

Peter Dreyer, *San Francisco Magazine,* 1974

"…the oldest and most successful poetry cooperative in the country."

Kenneth Lamott, "Poetry Here! Hot Off the Press," *The New York Times Magazine*, August 29, 1976

Contents

Foreword

This is a collection of essays/memoirs written by artists and poets about their experiences during the 1960s through the 1990s. There are thirty-three unique essays about what was happening in the culture and in personal lives. All are written by writers who were at some point members of the Berkeley Poets Cooperative. Each captures a sense of the tumultuous times.

It was a time when the universities were under attack and free speech was in question, when the byword of the culture rang out, "Question authority." But it was also a time when all of us were willing to come together and discuss such things as the worth of a word in a poem. Some narratives are long, some are short. One is simply a poem; others have poems interspersed throughout. One essay is a memorial celebration of a young fellow poet's short life. One writer discusses life in a commune. Another relates how the Berkeley Poets Cooperative community saved the author's life in a time of personal crisis. The memoirs form a patchwork quilt of a unique era. The intention is to share this amazing period in history, from the point of view of poets and writers who were there and lived the experience, and bring into focus "the way we were" in Berkeley, California, when everything seemed possible.

Why do it now? Nearly half a century since the founding of the Berkeley Poets Cooperative, the difficult times have returned. Since the bank failures, the collapse of Lehman Brothers, and the resulting Great Recession of 2007, we are experiencing a rise in poverty, a rise of the super-rich, the inequality of the 1% versus the 99%, and it feels as if the culture is beginning to fear the closing down of the "American dream." Mario Savio said in the late 1960s: "There's a time when the operation of the machine becomes so odious—makes you so sick at heart—that you can't take part. You can't even passively take part. And you've got to put your bodies upon the gears and upon the wheels, upon the levers, upon all the apparatus, and you've got to make it stop. And you've got to indicate to the people who run it, to the people who own it, that unless you're free, the machine will be prevented from working at all." Our society seems to have reached that point again, this time without the optimism of the 1960s and 1970s.

The essays in this collection remind us of a time when the spirit of cooperation was a force in the culture. People took matters into their own hands, working from the bottom up, a forerunner to the Occupy Movement. The phrase of the day was "Power to the people." The young writers who started The Berkeley Poets Cooperative decided to have a say-so about what was important in literature and in the culture. In the *Berkeley Monthly* (1976), Fred Cody wrote that the Berkeley Poets Cooperative was "a signpost to the future," and perhaps it was. Most of the poets who started in the Berkeley Poets Cooperative are still publishing, teaching, and sharing the gift of poetry. One thing this book suggests is that cooperatives can be successful organizations and offer an opportunity to break away from the top-down structures of the capitalist winner-take-all economy. These essays are testimonials to a way of life that emphasizes beauty and human enlightenment instead of quarterly profits and unequal distribution of wealth. A cooperative way of life. It still seems possible.

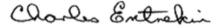

In the Beginning

I came to Berkeley at the age of 26 with $400 in my bank account in the summer of 1967, a widower with a three-year-old son, Demian, on the advice of my philosophy professor at the University of Alabama in Tuscaloosa: *Go west*, he said, *go to Berkeley. That's where it's happening.* I had a burning desire to be a writer, to study philosophy, to swim in a sea of thinkers and artists and writers. And Berkeley was where it was happening.

Charles Entrekin

1970

Issue #1 of the Berkeley Poets Cooperative magazine: original art and poetry and a comic strip

Contributors: Tom O'Rourke, Charles Entrekin, Maggie Entrekin, Ted Fleischman, Robert Gerstenlauer, Michael Perna, Rodham Tulloss

Cover Art: Maggie Entrekin

BPC Years: 1972–1975

THE POETS POOL
(reprinted from the *Daily Cal*, 1974)

Susan Stern

If you've heard of the Berkeley Poets Cooperative, it's probably because one day you tripped over someone selling the Co-op's magazine on Telegraph Avenue. The Co-op's been putting out a 68-page poetry-fiction-graphics magazine two times a year for about three years, and selling out the 2,000 copies of each issue mostly on the streets of Berkeley, so if you've been here for a while you've probably either bought some poetry from the Co-op or at least pushed the magazine out of your face a couple of times and continued walking.

The Poets Cooperative does not exist solely to publish the magazine. The magazine represents the best work to come out of the weekly poetry workshops, where anyone is invited to come, read their poetry, discuss their work with other poets, criticize other's work, drink too much coffee and inevitably disrupt things a little by crawling over everyone in search of the bathroom.

In order to understand what the Poets Co-op is, you have to examine the words we use to describe organizations of people.

First of all, the Poets Cooperative is a cooperative, not a collective. There is a difference. A collective tends to be an organization of people gathered to accomplish a set goal or program. The authority structure in a collective is not hierarchical. Set patterns for operations and work roles must be established, and transience of members must be minimal.

Poets Pool

As a cooperative, the Poets Co-op is *least* concerned with being an organization. Unlike a collective, the structure of the Poets Co-op evolves from changes in membership and emphasis. The magazine, the poetry readings at bookstores and coffee houses, and recently the beginning of a series of "chapbooks" (one-poet-books of 26 pages), are the result of poets pooling their resources.

In the Poets Cooperative, the idea of "membership" is not as simple as in a collective. For the type of work the collective must accomplish, the membership must be clearly defined. If you are a member of a collective, all the responsibilities and rewards of the collective apply to you.

However, in the Poets Co-op the word "member" is used to mean something else.

Members and Dismembers

It describes a certain type of involvement in the cooperative that is not desired by everyone or necessary to reap the rewards. The "members" of the Berkeley Poets Cooperative are a core group of about 15 people who have agreed to edit and publish the magazines, oversee the group's financial situation, answer correspondence, set up poetry readings, and generally make sure there is a place for the workshops to take place.

Not all the "members" come to all the workshops, and not all the members have their poetry published in the magazine, and the members aren't the same from issue to issue.

In addition, you don't have to be a "member" or work on the magazine to have your poetry published or read at one of the poetry readings. It is not unusual for "members" to "dis-member" themselves and continue to participate just in the workshops. The only difference is in what type of cooperation a person feels like being involved in: in sharing poetry and ideas at the workshops, or in publishing the magazines, or both.

The beauty of this organization is that it can include and benefit from the transience and diversity of its participants, and still maintain enough structure to perpetuate itself.

You Become It

There is no way of describing who makes up the Co-op. If you come to it you become it. "He who digs Los Angeles is Los Angeles," as Allen Ginsberg said. The people are poets. On the side they are sometimes students, or "street people" or dancers or waterbed salesmen or "wife-and-mothers" or computer programmers or primal therapists or short order cooks or professors.

The meetings take place crowded into someone's living room. There are no leaders or moderators, and no structure for the discussion, or rather the "happening."

Expect Anything

I've been going to the weekly workshop-meetings for two years now and all I've learned is not to have any expectations as to what will happen. Sometimes it's a small group of 10 people who all know each other, and the criticism is well thought-out and well-received, and there is a sense of the whole group participating in the creation of a poem and the growth of a poet. Sometimes the gathering is a crowd of 50 or more, with each person exhibiting striking personality and poetry, people just in from Michigan or New York or the ranch or just elsewhere. There have been times when people have sung their poetry, danced it, or encouraged everyone to chant it with them.

Sometimes the discussion is right out of a college creative writing class, and sometimes the criticism is highly technical. At times the whole cramped roomful is concentrating on listening to a poem or discussing a particular point, and sometimes the room is broken up into laughter, personal conversation, and general discussion of an experience found in the poem.

The Berkeley Poets Cooperative is a process and the real "members" are the people who join in that process any time for any length of time. The Berkeley Poets Cooperative is a poem being written, each line following from the next, spontaneously and true to form.

1971

Contributors: Rona Spalten, Charles Entrekin, Bruce Hawkins, Maggie Entrekin, Chuck Cohen, Bruce Boston, Maggie Cloherty, Clive Matson, Rodham Elliott Tulloss, Maribelle Freeman, Ted Fleischman, Anne Hawkins.

Cover: Anne Hawkins
Artwork: Maggie Entrekin

2207 OREGON STREET

Charles Entrekin

In 1968, having been hired as a trainee in a new profession, computer programming, I met and married my son's nursery school teacher, Karen Marie Keenan, who, like many artists in Berkeley, worked days to pay for evening classes at the College of Arts & Crafts. First conversation I had with her, she informed me, "Your son says he wants to marry me." After we married, she changed her name to Maggie Entrekin, less conventional, more artistic, and we rented a two-story house, an aging brown shingle in South Berkeley. And it was there that we held the first meeting of the Berkeley Poets Cooperative.

Our new home, 2207 Oregon Street, was in a borderline, mixed neighborhood, across from Le Conte grammar school with its paved playgrounds and basketball courts, but it was sandwiched between exciting Telegraph Avenue and business-oriented Shattuck Avenue, and it offered easy access to campus, and close proximity to the Free University of Berkeley and the newly formed Free Clinic. It was an ideal location.

Our first issue had, as its cover, a black and white, expressionist pen and ink wash of a giant, newly pregnant woman, by Maggie Entrekin. Looking back now, I can see it was perfectly symbolic. It was a self-portrait, but it was also about the times. The culture was electric with possibilities. In 1969 Woodstock happened; the first moon landing took place; Vietnam anti-war protests were growing; in Berkeley, the Free Speech movement was part of our world view, our *Weltanschauung*; *The Berkeley Barb*, sold on the streets, became the People's newspaper; and it was in 1969 that the Berkeley Poets Cooperative was officially founded, the same year the Free Clinic was founded, People's Park was being "occupied," and anti-war marches and demonstrations were ongoing. And then, in 1969, Ronald Reagan, who thought that UC Berkeley was "a haven for communist sympathizers, protesters and sex deviants," first called out the state police and then, finally, the National Guard. The city was put under curfew. One student was shot and killed by the police; hundreds of Berkeley citizens were hospitalized. Police helicopters sprayed tear gas over the campus. Over 30,000 Berkeley citizens marched against Reagan's take-over of the City of Berkeley.

In the midst of all this *sturm und drang*, we poets and artists and writers declared ourselves a cooperative and set about self-publishing our first issue of the *Berkeley Poets Cooperative*.

We found an offset printer for issue one in a run-down, two-story condemned house on Shattuck Avenue. A fast talking, friendly young man met us in the doorway and told us they'd print, collate, and staple-bind 500 copies for $169, half up front, and half on delivery, in one week's time. But we weren't allowed inside their print shop. They were moving. We had to trust them, based on hand-out samples of their work. It was a good price. We agreed to trust them. But when I showed up a week later, the house seemed empty.

And then I heard some noise coming from the street level basement at the side of the house. Squeezing past a broken, unpainted wooden gate, I discovered an open window and peered down into the darkened basement. Inside, there was a lot of commotion as young people seemed to be running around, shouting, hurry-up in their voices. Tension was in the air. But then one of them recognized me and came over to the window. No, we couldn't come in, but if I had the final payment in cash, he'd pass the 500 copies out through the window. I paid him, and we had our first issue of *The Berkeley Poets Cooperative*.

The word I received from second-hand sources was that Issue #1 was printed on stolen government envelope stock. Our printer was the secretive Weather Underground, founded in, guess what year, 1969, as a faction of SDS (Students for a Democratic Society), and supposedly dedicated to the overthrow of the US Government. Less than a year later the house was gone, as was all trace of the people who printed Issue #1. At 50 cents a copy, we sold out all 500 copies.

Having lost our printer but committed to going forward, we first toyed with the idea of putting the Co-op under the auspices of the Free University of Berkeley. But after a few tries at meeting with the staff of the Free U., we decided it would not work. The biggest reason: we wanted a free and open workshop where everyone could voice an opinion and where what mattered was the work itself, where the work had to stand on its own, with strengths and weaknesses exposed. The idea was that we wanted to build a workshop organized around honest feedback so that we, as writers, could grow and improve. The Free U. staff wanted a more controlled, more directed, professor-to-student environment. So we parted ways.

We opened our doors to all comers and began planning Issue #2. One of our members, Clive Matson, wanted to purchase a letterpress and for the rest of us to learn the art of letterpress printing. He agreed to take over the whole production effort, at no cost to us, if we would agree to purchase the required type sets and help with setting of the type and the running of the letterpress. It was delicate, hard work, but we did it, plate by plate, page by page, with ink-stained fingers and hands, with coarse brown paper stock that soaked up the ink, and with tiny bits of cardboard forcing the leveling of each character on the plate's bound page, its *forme*. It was a labor of love, but it was a one-time effort. Each page had to be broken down and reformed. There would be no reprints. With a bold, almost flag-waving salmon-pink cover, new poems, and delicate pen-and-ink line drawings of nudes, we tripled our retail price to $1.50, and, once again, sold out all 500 copies.

We were getting recognized locally and nationally, with a reputation for quality, and we were doing it outside of academia. We were beginning to take ourselves seriously. And so, in 1971, we began the long debate as to the nature of what it meant to be a member of the Berkeley Poets Cooperative. Bruce Hawkins puts the Co-op's cultural perspective in verse on the copyright page of Issue #4:

> Bullshit is much like quicksand
> for those who are caught in it
> but a very obliging quicksand
> which never gets deep enough
> to cover the mouth
> that's making it.

The Co-op was not about ideology, not about personality, not about politics. It was about the work.

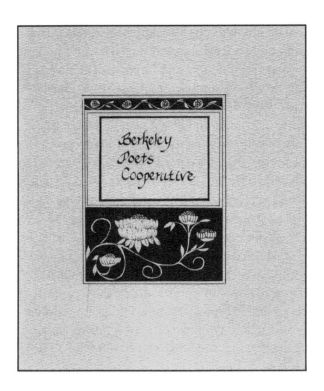

1971

Issue #3 Contributors: Rodham Elliott Tulloss, Kathleen Raven, Bruce Hawkins, Charles Entrekin, Peter Weissman, Richard Wyatt, Ron Schreiber, Rona Spalten, Chuck Cohen, Clive Matson, Susan K. Levin, Ted Fleischman, Mike Helm, Blanche Madiol, Stan Krohmer, Greg Dunn, Bruce Boston.

Artwork: Maggie Entrekin

BEING THERE

Rodham Tulloss

Driving north from the Bay Bridge on the East Bay Freeway, the mudflats at low tide were decorated with giant figures, huts, abstractions nailed together from planks washed in from the outer world and decorated with abandoned tires. I was living in low-income housing in Richmond (a tax break for some large corporation), conveniently near a Cal field station from which I could take a shuttle bus to the Cal campus, where I was enrolled in the Group for Logic and Methodology of Science. For lunch, I often ate a street vendor's brown rice with as much of the free scallions, sesame seeds, and soy sauce as I could fit into the Styrofoam bowl. There was a Japanese restaurant on the north side of campus where the chefs rolled up caramelized (burnt) rice layers from inside their rice cookers, sliced it into spirals about three-quarters of an inch thick, and set it out for patrons to take for free. I ate quite a bit of that when I arrived at the right time.

It was 1969—Vietnam War, famous photo of a helicopter dropping tear gas over the Campanile, People's Park in its early days, County Sheriff's department under direct control of Ronald Reagan, the great sweep of Shattuck Avenue arresting even the shoppers and mail carriers (one of whom—a federal employee, mind you—was a neighbor of mine with diabetes who was beaten until his shoes were full of blood), sometimes so much tear gas in campus buildings that classes were held outside. The student health service dispensed Thorazine as an "anxiety titrate" with advice to take as much as necessary to suppress the mental pain. They failed to inform us that the drug was addictive and that we'd experience debilitating visual and tactile hallucinations if we suddenly stopped taking it. My first child was born that October in Berkeley...a natural childbirth in the midst of war, personal and societal chaos, and, "Find the true peace within, man."

Tom O'Rourke, who had a second floor apartment on the opposite side of the tax write-off complex, suggested we go together to a group in Berkeley, a developing workshop, in which he was reading and hearing poetry. I had sworn that I would do nothing but grad school, set aside poetry and other things, get practical. But it probably took Tom less than an hour to get me interested in this group in Berkeley. We went to the next workshop—Charles Entrekin's house at 2207 Oregon. I just remembered how odd it seemed to me then that, in Berkeley, people didn't ever append "street" or "avenue" to some names such as "Oregon."

That group became the Berkeley Poets Co-operative (hyphenated only on the cover of the first two issues of the magazine and always without an apostrophe) and, from very near the beginning, included fiction writers as well as poets. I joined up near the beginning of the Co-op—one of the six original members. People "joined" by showing up for the meetings and persisting. I persisted until I had to leave Berkeley to find a job in the East, in the summer of 1971.

For a period of less than three years, living under politico-socio-emotional duress, I was part of one of the most satisfying and good-humored professional relationships of my life. My colleagues in the Berkeley Poets Cooperative judged my writing, not me. We wrote and learned, and we taught each other. We were deadly serious about writing; we tried to speak truth; and we laughed a lot. It is still, in my mind, a near ideal of a collaborative, which has been my preferred mode of work in every profession that I've had since. It was entirely nontoxic, organic, but possibly flammable. Given the basics of survival (it sure as hell didn't produce cash), it was a great way for a young person to learn to work; and it felt like play. My memories of the Co-op are dominated by the poems that I most enjoyed and have read and reread many times; by the persisting memory of openness, friendship, community, and interactive creativity that so delighted me; and the relaxed comfort of the Entrekins' living room.

I recall the first time I realized that a poem was failing because the author was not aware that the words created an emotional score and that, after reaching a point of some intensity, he had neglected the score rather suddenly, producing lines that seemed to lay down their instruments and leave the session. I remember drawing curves graphing the supposed emotional score of poems in order to better communicate during some discussions at the Co-op.

Once, in a burst of...something, someone declared forcefully that we must all write poems with the last line "The revolution is coming." At least one such poem (Charles Entrekin, *BPC #2*, p. 9) was duly written and preceded on page 8 of the same magazine by a poem of which the main image involved the aforementioned East Bay mudflats; I discovered in rereading the poems that I had conflated the two poems in memory.

There was an evening when someone broke the news that the manufacturers of Red Mountain Wine were going to have to remove the word "wine" from their label because it was manufactured from alcohol tinged with a grape-juice-like additive.

One night Charles, Bruce Hawkins, Bruce Boston, and I were photographed in front of Charles's fireplace...all sporting significant beards and long or longish hair. I had that photograph over my desk at Bell Laboratories for my entire twenty-five years there. More than once, some manager asked me who the "anarchists" were. To steal a pitch from the old Boys' Town fund raising letters: They ain't anarchists, Boss. They're my brothers.

I remember a big party at Charles's house (perhaps it was a wedding celebration?). I had nothing with which to buy a present so I gave an afternoon and evening of cooking tempura. We went through every vegetable and fruit in the house to deal with a massive epidemic of the munchies. Finally, the only thing left was a stack of watermelon rinds from which the fruit had been entirely removed. I made the watermelon rinds into tempura; every bit was eaten.

I wish I could remember more. I decided to go through the early issues again, starting with the first issue with Maggie Entrekin's, broad-brushed, black-ink-wash sketch of a pregnant torso on the otherwise white cover...of an issue including (in addition to another wash and a line drawing, both Maggie's) only poems of the original six male poets. That issue sold for fifty cents. I was surprised to see that the index of the issue lists an "introduction" on page 4, very probably written by Charles, who was the natural spokesman and sole official of the Co-op from the beginning—on a laid back and as needed basis. As I started to read the unsuspecting official preface to the coming decades of workshops, magazines, and chapbooks, its relaxed, unpretentious simplicity came back to me—the voice of an old, dear friend:

"BERKELEY POETS CO-OPERATIVE exists as a vehicle for the publication of poetry and other graphic art. As such, the magazine embodies no philosophy, artistic or otherwise, except that which arises naturally from the more or less close association of the people involved in its production.

"The poets and artists represented here worked together in many ways, first in an informal workshop and later in the actual production of the magazine.

"That's how it goes. If you're interested in contributing to the magazine and willing to help publish it—time thought materials money—contact Charles Entrekin. [postal address]."

I have an isolated memory of being told that the fly-by-night printer of *BPC* #1 said it was printed on "stolen envelope stock."

Some of the poets seemed to me then to have already developed unique voices—something I greatly envied because my poems of the period (especially as I see them now) often seem to be catalogs of easily discernible influences. I can see the already extant, strong narrative element in Charles's work in the first issue of the *Berkeley Poets Co-operative* (1970). He's dealing with some pieces of his past in Alabama and elsewhere; the tragedies that found him too early in life; and his young adulthood lived in part in the brutal years of official, police, and Klan resistance to the American Civil Rights movement. Years later, many of these elements appeared fully fleshed in his novel about those times—*Red Mountain, Birmingham, Alabama, 1965.*

After the first issue, we had a sort of crisis of identity. Could we continue? We heard of a new workshop in town east of Telegraph Avenue and decided to offer to merge with that group. We told them we had a small amount of money, some unsold issues of a magazine, and a core group of writers. But what we perceived as a gift was not accepted. I remember that we thought maybe we had been a bit too sudden or had been too much involved in the details of writing for a new group to accept at such an early stage in its development. Somehow, we had an air of knowing what we were doing after only about one year of our collaborative process. Maybe, we flattered ourselves, we had really matured and learned how to teach and learn. We probably had made a significant start on the creation of the future Cooperative. At the same time, several vigorous new voices joined

BPC. I'm not sure if they all came from the other group; but I think at least one did, explaining that he/she felt we seemed to do our best to give useful criticism and discussion and that that was more supportive than a diet of pats on the back. The new writers and the increased confidence that we were actually doing something that at least some other groups did not do and doing it well enough to have other writers recognize us as a resource, led us to abandon the idea of merging into some other process.

The second issue of the *Berkeley Poets Co-operative* (1971, priced originally at $1.50) is marked by the first appearance of new voices that strengthened and diversified the Cooperative. In this number, the following appear for the first time: Rona Spalten ("my body/ flowers incessantly"), Bruce Hawkins (nine short poems coming from some place in the mind where I had never been), Bruce Boston (represented by a segment of his novel, *Stained Glass Rain*), and Clive Matson (represented by one poem). All had long associations with the Co-op. Anne Hawkins did the cover. Charles, Ted Fleischman, and I were the writers carrying over from the first issue; and Maggie again contributed illustrations.

Number two was the last issue that was published during my time in Berkeley. *BPC* #3 is dated "fall, 1971" and includes a political poem I remember writing in Princeton that year. That seems unbelievable to me! I so strongly identified myself with the group that I thought I had been in Berkeley for five or six issues; but that is only a very slightly interesting fact about my memory and the reflection in that false memory of the importance to me of the brother/sisterhood of the Berkeley Poets Co-op.

1972

Contributors: Russ Leong, Bruce Hawkins, Rachel Nahem, Charles Entrekin, Kara Schmidt, Patricia Ann Treat, Rosemary Christoph, Mal Coffino, Charles Klein, Naomi Lowinsky, Doris P. Morrison, Judith Stone, Bartolome Alberti, Rodham Elliott Tulloss, Pearl Bates, John Gardner, Michael Helm, Kathleen Raven, Howard Berglund, Ted Fleischman, Scott Lowell, Maggie Entrekin, Lynda Koolish, Vaclav E. Benes, Leah Phol, Evelyn Hoye.

Layout/design: Gary A. Head
Calligraphy: Marion Sirefman

BPC Years: 1969–?

THE ERA OF MARTIN LUTHER KING HAD COME AND GONE

Ted Fleischman

One day, soon after we started the Berkeley Poets Co-op, Charles announced that we had an opportunity to publish broadsides. So I thought, what trees will we staple these broadsides to? No shit, that's really what I thought. And it was a bummer, the era of Martin Luther King had come and gone.

Despite that, Charles gave us plenty of reasons to leap into the project. Semi-unrecognized artists would illustrate the broadsides and pretty good printers would roll them off their silkscreen presses. Not a chance that any would hang in a museum, but we might get some in restaurants.

We had a broadside party with many, many people. I think that was a turning point for the Berkeley Poets Co-op.

***

I really don't have much interest in looking backward. It's useful to remember — sometimes, but not often. The past is, at best, a ghost and, at worst, an addiction.

***

We ran the Berkeley Poets Co-op like a business. I was in the marketing department. We were the keepers of the Berkeley Poets Co-op (BPC) and Berkeley Poets Workshop and Press (BPW&P) brands. For maybe a dozen years, we pitched BPW&P products to the California Arts Council, the National Endowment for the Arts, Squaw Valley Writers' Conference, KPFA, and innumerable bookstores like Cody's and Kepler's, where our reps read their poetry from our publications.

I also lent a helping hand to the legal and sales groups. But sales really was, first and last, Bruce Hawkins. He was nonpareil. I think people knew Bruce and loved his poetry first, and the fact he would sell his fans the Berkeley Poets Co-op Magazine was secondary.

We could have called ourselves the Berkeley Poets Commune or the Berkeley Poetry Commune, if those names had not already been claimed. We all worked in the production line, which were our monthly workshops. If we weren't constantly building poems, it was short stories, or even a short play. But like good communists, we all believed that we all owned the means of production and the copyright was simply legal cover to allow us to deal with the stinking poetry capitalist cartels back East and elsewhere.

But none of us were communists. We mostly had jobs and didn't share the wealth or attend rallies for Gus Hall. I might be incorrect, maybe some of us did and didn't discuss that stuff.

We even were kind of hypnotized by the Protestant Ethic, where you work hard at writing and that's that. We even were kind of hypnotized, too, by capitalism, where anyone could be a successful business owner, and the BPW&P was a business.

Were we ambitious and seeking success or fame? I think we did, and for those ends we needed a great CEO, and the BPW&P had the best CEO ever, Charles Entrekin. Charles was a terrific writer and critic and managed corporate strategy superbly and subtly. He brought the pieces together and we all helped with the glue. Maybe you could say, the BPW&P was both a poetry workshop and glue factory.

HALF A BOTTLE OF CATSUP

I know.
I am sulking
You know
what it seems to be.
A bottle of catsup
I am the catsup
across from,
slouched on the front room sofa.
Aunt Martha's holy picture
smiles down on me.
But can I help it?
Please put me the pantry.
Close the door.
I want to be left alone.

—*From* Half a Bottle of Catsup *(BPW&P)*

BERKELEY POETS COOPERATIVE
Number Five

1973

Contributors: Rona Spalten, Bruce Boston, Michael Helm, Judith Stone, Lawrence Burke, Rod Tulloss, Laurel Taylor, Charles Entrekin, Bruce Hawkins, Dennis Anderson, Jennifer Stone, Crysta Casey, Susan Stern, Ted Fleischman, Harry Wuldman, Lucille Day, Michael Helm, Kathleen Raven, Ken McKeon, Charles Klein, Ann Hawkins, Maggie Entrekin, Diane Hofberg.

Cover: Russ Leong
Layout: Gary Head
Calligraphy: Maggie Entrekin

CHANGE IN THE AIR

Clive Matson

The brown shingle Victorian where the Berkeley Poets Cooperative met was slightly run-down, left over from an elegant age, but very comfortable and unpretentious. Up a wide porch with wooden stairs, through an entrance hall and we entered a generous living room with dark wainscoting. The walls had surely witnessed discussions, passionate discussions, and had survived. That made the house a perfect setting. Charles Entrekin and the writers around him welcomed my friends and me with game smiles and wary eyes.

It was 1970 and the Co-op had been around a few years. The group was probably no stranger to Shelley's proclamation, "Poets are the unacknowledged legislators of the world." But if they were strangers, that would change. All kinds of change was in the air. We were sure poetry was the foundation of how people think, and this made poems the cells with which humankind builds itself. What we wrote might be a vibrant field in the greening of America. And the Co-op's work could be so powerful that poets would finally earn their proper acknowledgment.

We were going to work out the destiny of our culture through the Co-op. As a thought, and nothing more, that's a huge burden for any group. Did the organizers sense this, and did they have some idea what was coming? I'm reminded of a poet who, after achieving fame, went to India and this seemed an enlightened trip. But he confessed in his journals, later, that he went as a complete rube. He had no plan and no idea what was there. The organizers probably had no plan, either, and started the Co-op because it seemed like a cool thing to do. Why not? It fit the ethos of the time. What's notable is how steadfastly the Co-op held to the ideal.

It was valuable that newcomers entered, were included in the group, and felt on equal footing. How valuable? Compare a University of California at Riverside poetry group a few years before, where a professor quietly and respectfully revealed that "gray ash-tray room" was the sort of image poets were writing those days. He spoke kindly to a group of students, eager students, who adroitly displayed their intelligence in hopes of joining a special society. For the professor, the poets were unreachable and arcane. For the students, the poets were as remote as the Mindanao Trench. In contrast, the Berkeley Poets Cooperative was, well, priceless.

Consider also Josephine Miles who, at the same time, in the 1970s, must have been throwing open her Berkeley house, though I didn't attend until later. A crowd of students gathered at her feet and gave dutiful respect. They read poems and Miles gave feedback that seemed insightful and generous. She encouraged all manner of risks, personal, aesthetic, and political, but there was nothing to discuss. She had position in the poetry world and supported her work with a body of thought, as one often does in the academy, on "Structuralism." There were no issues, certainly no burning issues. Her world seemed established and secure.

I don't remember much in 1970 that was established and secure. I'd come from two years with Berkeley's Taxi Unlimited, a producers' cooperative, and couldn't make a living wage. I'm not sure anyone there could; most of the workers were on some form of relief, and supported the company as much as the company supported us. But the meetings were a vibrant stew of idealistic proposals. We were sure, if we articulated anarchist or socialist values clearly and acted in accordance, that the company would survive. And it would make money. During our fervent sessions we'd see our ideals foundering under waves of conflicting views. But our thinking got sharper in the process. What were our ideals, and how should they be formulated?

Taxi challenged what I'd been doing. Discussions there brought my political background to the fore and I applied it to my writing. A few years before, from 1960 to 1968 in New York City, I'd been in the star system. There was no doubt who was God in the poetry world, although, if you looked around, you'd see a bunch of gods. But one's effort, universally, was to get close to your personal star and have some of the glamour rub off. If your opinion was different from mine, and mine was shared by John Wieners, then you were beyond the pale. Alden Van Buskirk wrote, "Fuck Olson and the crowd. For me only Ginsb., McClure, and Wieners." That was how I felt, and that gave me some of Van Buskirk's extreme cool.

The Berkeley Poets Cooperative hadn't heard of Wieners, let alone Van Buskirk. I should certainly explain what was missing. Hunker down sniffing amphetamine and eating donuts, stay up all night several nights in a row, read their texts over and over, then take lysergic acid and see if your visions match. But it's certain the Co-op wasn't disposed quite that kindly toward the Beats. And I did have just enough social graces not to inflict such a demanding idea on people who were, overall, gracious and accepting. But personally, as for my writing, was I still in the star system? Mix in the communism of my family and my efforts in cooperation at Taxi, what would likely come up? Quite a stressful internal battle, and the tension spilled into the Co-op. Charles and his friends could, no doubt, feel the energy shaking that house. Maintaining composure, for all of us, was a struggle.

How do you write poetry, which is too often seen as an elite enterprise, and communicate democratically? And what, after all, is democratic communication? People write for a variety of reasons, as the Co-op demonstrated. One, to look good for our peers and to impress others with our intelligence. Another, to guide the reader into a vision and share an interesting journey. And of course, to promote political and social ideals. Still other reasons: to entertain, or to justify, or for revenge, and this is only the beginning. We were each doing one or two or three of these, to some extent, and that's difficult to admit. More difficult to talk about. We didn't know how. Discussions went on after the Co-op meetings, with me, Chuck Cohen, Raven, and Peter Weismann. How do you stay true to your insight and, at the same time, be a good Co-op member?

The Co-op was set up to operate cooperatively, as a magazine, and this cooperative spirit spilled over to include some aesthetics. Or so we assumed. We voted on what to publish and how to publish, and we gave each other more or less equal time and equal respect. But the voting shook down as if the group were an oligarchy. An unconscious oligarchy. What group, this side of the Brazilian highlands, would not fit this description? So many listened to Charles. And they should, it's natural. He was the steady one, he dealt with contention well, the group was central to his life. He held the cooperative space.

But strong feelings did make the group uncomfortable. That puts in the margins a pretty wide swath of English and American poetry and, in that house, outrageous politics wouldn't fly, either. We invited Raven to the Co-op anyway. Where else could she go? With flaming black hair and bugged-out eyes and a carbide-hard assurance that her words, taken in good faith, would turn the world upside-down? Of course, the Berkeley Poets Cooperative would understand. It's remarkable that they let her in the door. And Peter Weismann, with his shoulders hunched and tensed toward righting the wrongs of the Jewish people with a fervor that wouldn't stay in his shirt. The Co-op, where else? The newspapers weren't going to listen.

You see the problem. To keep some cooperative spirit viable and healthy was not easy. And discussions spin out when instincts come into play. The Co-op revered Robert Bly, and when you tune in to whoever speaks to your soul, Shakespeare or Wieners or Van Buskirk, and know yourself captivated, how do you keep your mouth shut? Discussions about equality stop dead in their tracks. The equality we want is to discover the secrets of the greats and equal their power. Then capture a bit of immortality. If the reason they write fits one of those sleazy categories, and it does, that would be embarrassing. Bit by bit, over the months, I came from the discussions with a formulation that could be true overall, as I edited my political manuscript, *On The Inside*. "Poetry is a vehicle for consciousness."

The structure Charles set up bent, and bent, and bent, and stayed intact. The Co-op accommodated strong opinions, from bohemians and extreme feminists and tooth-spitting radicals. Most of us were published, though we found that milder pieces had a better chance of being accepted. But they had a chance of being accepted. Charles had help with the dissonance from Ted Fleischman and Bruce Boston, though they both had strong opinions and it's hard to be cooperative at the same time. Charles managed. He had support, too, from Bruce Hawkins, the soft-spoken baseball fan, who defied the political radicals with his book LESS POWER, showing a weak light bulb on the front cover. The book contained lovely lyrics, and he was the most respected poet in the group.

Who came through the Co-op? Many interesting writers, Lucy Day, Ken Knabb, and Alicia Ostriker and Rod Tulloss, who became East Coast outposts when they moved. The Poets Co-op was a learning place for writers, a place to learn how to publish and how to deal with each other. There were joint activities. For a while we even played basketball on the courts of the Le Conte Middle School on nearby Fulton Street. Of course, there were also failures. The walls absorbed the conflicts that arose and were left hanging. Karen Brodine was a favorite of mine. If a man violated her space with a look suggesting she was property, it was reason to aim her car at him and threaten his body. But Charles got her published, too. He'd probably say he didn't, but he set up the structure and held us to it. That made things happen.

Behind those conflicts was the ache of not knowing my own aesthetic. Or how it fit the world and society. Behind that ache was a yearning to find out, a yearning for a forum where it could be discovered and refined. When your aesthetic matches the need of the culture or some part of it, you're blessed. But I do think the message of those discussions is that when you're deep in your process, you don't really know what's going on. You go on. And the aesthetic is fluid. We're not supposed to have an unchanging aesthetic.

Is it forty-some years later? The issues are not resolved, and there's no imperative, outside of my wish, that they should be resolved. But Occupy has brought them up again. Who is the one-percent, and how can we reach them? Or how can we effectively reach the ninety-nine percent? What does the phrase mean, the one that Occupy uses, "direct democracy"? Should it apply to our writing? And when we understand that our subtext, as we present a position, may convey, "Stay where you are," as easily as, "Turn your world upside-down," the discussion gets really complicated.

This recalls our debates of the early 1970s that went nowhere. We just continued. And the Co-op continued, following Charles across town, then to various places, and into this century at an early member's home. I'd like to drive by that first house on the south side, if I could find it, and see if it still exists, if the walls still stand. We wouldn't want to paint them with nostalgia. But it would be inspiring if the house were simply there.

We need the debate. You might have noticed the web breeds its own aesthetic, one that's brief, shallow, and unconscious. This cries out for more and better discussion, as does Occupy, and the web makes debate more possible and less noticeable. Charles asks for this history and, knowing Charles, he's asking in the spirit of the Co-op. He'll give equal footing to everyone, as best he can, and likely he'll take all comers. This will show the virtue of taking all comers. It may not look coherent when the pieces stand side by side, and they may be painful, but the picture conveyed just might be complete. This makes the value of the enterprise inestimable.

"The taming power of the small" could be the salient line from the *I Ching*. To keep a cooperative spirit alive isn't, on the surface, world-shaking. But when everything around is changing, moving back into that ideal *is* a sort of change. And my sense is that, when change does happen, it's tiny. I move only a half inch, but that half inch is crucial. That small move engenders a new angle of sight, and everything looks different.

Then everything does change. That's huge.

A POET IS SOMEONE WHO STANDS OUTSIDE

Michael Helm

I was twenty-six when I first arrived in Berkeley in December of 1968 as a consequence of being promoted to the editorial staff of Wadsworth Publishing Company. I had spent the previous two-and-a-half years, since graduating from San Fernando Valley State College (now called California State University, Northridge), working out of Seattle as a traveling college textbook salesman in the Pacific Northwest. My job while there was to get Wadsworth books adopted for a variety of undergraduate courses, especially in math, English and psychology. This involved tracking down junior faculty, who taught most of the undergraduate courses, as well as talking with their key teaching assistants, most of whom were poorly paid graduate students trying to complete their Ph.D. requirements while avoiding the Vietnam War draft.

In general, my life on the road was an enjoyable one. After working hours, some of my evenings were spent in the company of younger, hipper staff with whom I drank red wine, smoked some grass, discussed the war and politics of the counterculture, and listened to Jimi Hendrix, the Electric Prunes, Dylan, the Doors, the Stones, and the Beatles. Other, more frequent evenings, I would grab a quick meal and repair back to my motel room where, depending upon my mood, I inhaled the fiction of Henry Miller, Charles Bukowski, Sherwood Anderson, and John Dos Passos or savored the Imagist poetry of Ezra Pound and T.S. Eliot, the hothouse poems of Theodore Roethke, or the inimitable wit of A. E. Housman and e.e. cummings. Occasionally, I would be inspired to work on a poem of my own, influenced by the creative writing classes I had taken with James Dickey in 1965–66 while he was the visiting poet-in-residence at Valley State.

Moving to Berkeley

Bidding farewell to the Pacific Northwest, I looked forward to my new Bay Area assignment for Wadsworth, which was to identify and sign contracts for innovative text projects from the undergraduate curriculum at UC Berkeley, Stanford, UC Santa Cruz, San Francisco State, and Cal State Hayward.

My first important decision, upon arriving in the Bay Area, was choosing where to live. I had driven down from Seattle and pulled into San Francisco on a cold and damp evening at the height of the Hong Kong Flu pandemic. It didn't take long for me to appreciate why Mark Twain had allegedly said the coldest winter he had ever spent was a summer in San Francisco. Chilled to the bone, I eschewed Herb Caen's mythical Baghdad by the Bay and drove east over the Bay Bridge, to what I hoped would be a balmier Berkeley micro-climate.

I spent my first night in Berkeley at an inexpensive motel on University Avenue, in front of which a couple of high-heeled, mini-skirted hookers intermittently paraded their booties. Since I didn't know anyone, my initial plan, before checking out the rental section in the latest copy of the *Berkeley Barb,* was to contact a local reference that had been given me by Dick Nash, a friend and fellow Northwest bookman who worked for Scott Foresman. Dick's reference, I discovered the next day, would turn out to be serendipitous. She was a Berkeley librarian by the name of Lowell who had just accepted a better-paying position in Phoenix and was about to move there. We hit it off and, after meeting with her the next day, Lowell offered to sublet her two-bedroom flat to me for a year, with the proviso that, if things didn't work out for her in Arizona, she could reclaim it.

The flat was located in a redline section of south Berkeley, above the Black and White Liquor store at the corner of Adeline and Emerson, and was available for the almost unbelievable rent of sixty dollars a month. Unlikely to find a better deal, I opted to live in the People's Republic of Berkeley, in favor of serendipity and cheap rent.

Since I couldn't move into her flat until after the first of the year, Lowell suggested I check out the International House on Piedmont Avenue, which rented rooms by the week to people who had business to do with the University. *Thank God,* I thought, *for friends and friends of friends.* I moved into the I-House hostel for the next three weeks, during which time, and beyond, it rained heavily for a record forty three consecutive days. Along with a daily drenching, I, of course, managed to soon catch the dreaded Hong Kong Flu, which kept me in bed, with alternating fever and chills, for five straight days. Fortunately, I recovered without any of the dangerous pulmonary complications that would cost over a million Asian people their lives that winter.

Over the next few months, I settled into my new, semi-bohemian life in Berkeley. My weekdays at UC Berkeley primarily consisted of researching the undergraduate curriculum, then meeting with the appropriate faculty, while dodging the occasional cloud of tear gas that would envelop student protestors at Sproul Plaza, the South Campus free-speech area. Alternately, my weekends were spent on Telegraph Avenue happily browsing through Moe's huge collection of used fiction and poetry, after which I would nurse a cappuccino and people-watch from the sidewalk tables that were situated across the street, in front of Caffé Mediterraneum.

Telegraph Avenue, like much of south Berkeley in the late 1960s and early 1970s, had a decidedly Indian flavor. Posters and tapestries of Indian deities and Kama Sutra positions hung from bedroom walls. Sitar and sarod ragas by Ravi Shankar and Ali Akbar Khan hypnotically twanged and permeated the air. A vibrant throng of rainbow people wore colorful tie-dyed t-shirts and madras skirts and shawls, patched blue jeans, and draw-string cotton pants. Stoned hippies reeked of patchouli and cannabis. Head-shaven, peach-robed Hare Krishnas chanted … *Hareh Krishna… Hareh Krishna… Hareh Rama…Hareh Krishna…* as they snaked their way through the crowd. Street vendors hawked inexpensive silver-and-turquoise jewelry, garnets, and lapis lazuli. Poet and bubble lady Julia Vinograd sold her latest chapbook on the street and in cafés.

People's Park

Then, over a three-week period in April and May of 1969, passions over People's Park erupted. In response to an April 18th *Berkeley Barb* article by Yippie Party co-founder Stew Albert, as well as subsequent campus rallies, more than 1,000 Berkeley residents, students, and merchants ultimately became involved in the building of the Park. Park activists pointed out that the University had used its power of eminent domain to acquire the 2.8 acre plot of land in 1967 for student housing. It then promptly evicted the residents and demolished all the houses, before running out of development money. In response to criticism, the University announced a change in plans that now involved building a student parking lot and soccer field on the site. Meanwhile, the situation became even more complicated. Without the necessary funds to complete the project, the University had left much of the debris from the demolition on the site, which attracted others to use it as a dump, creating an eyesore. Park activists proclaimed a higher, more attractive use for the site.

I was having my cappuccino at Caffé Med around noon on Sunday, April 20th, when one of the Park organizers came into the café and called out that a flatbed truck loaded with sod donated by Barbara Moskowitz had just arrived and that volunteers were needed to unload it. Curious to see what was happening, I, along with a dozen or so other individuals from the café, went around the corner, a block up Haste to Bowditch, where the truck was double-parked. Someone handed me a shovel and suggested that I join those who were already laying down the sod.

I paused for a moment to take in the scene. There were around 100 volunteers variously laying sod, planting flowers, shrubs and trees, while a dozen or so Berkeley Police, apparently content to laugh and smirk, watched us work. Feeling empowered, I worked for a couple of hours at the east end of the Park before calling it quits. Over the next three weeks, People's Park supporters contributed enough labor, money, and materials to convert the ugly, vacant lot into a functioning park.

But activists had initiated a seizure of University property that Ronald Reagan was determined to squash. So it was that, at 4:30 a.m. on May 15th, Reagan sent in some 300 California Highway Patrol and Berkeley police officers with orders to destroy the Park and erect an 8-foot-tall perimeter chain-link fence to keep everyone out.

By early afternoon, more than 3,000 protesters had moved to retake the Park and were met by the remaining force of 159 Berkeley and University police officers. Fire hydrants were opened, rocks and bottles were thrown, and the fence attacked by protesters, while the police fired off tear-gas canisters in an unsuccessful attempt to disperse the crowd.

Unhappy with the escalating violence and unwilling to risk having my skull cracked open, I retreated from the immediate area and watched, as more police arrived from surrounding cities, as well as a contingent of shotgun-toting Alameda County Sheriff's deputies. This increased the number of police to some 791 officers in full riot gear (helmets, shields, and gas masks) who by then faced some 6,000 protesters.

The officers, under Ronald Reagan's Chief of Staff Ed Meese's command, waded into the tear-gassed crowd with flailing nightsticks, while several of the Alameda deputies indiscriminately fired their shotguns at protestors, some of whom had congregated on nearby rooftops. James Rector was fatally injured and Alan Blanchard permanently blinded, and at least 128 protesters were admitted to local hospitals for head trauma, shotgun wounds, and other serious injuries. Meanwhile, according to the University of California Police Department, 111 officers suffered comparatively minor injuries, although one deputy was allegedly stabbed in the chest.

Events further escalated when Reagan declared a state of emergency, leading to the two-week occupation of Berkeley by some 2,700 National Guardsmen. The Guardsmen, with fixed bayonets and rifles at the ready, quickly established a four-block perimeter surrounding the Park and threw up checkpoints at numerous street intersections to close off access to the park site. Meanwhile, Berkeley Police enthusiastically embraced the task of heavy-handedly enforcing an early evening curfew throughout south and west Berkeley. Things came to a conclusion on May 30th, when some 30,000 Berkeley residents peacefully protested the National Guard's occupation, which ended soon thereafter.

The Berkeley Poets Co-op

My first contact with the Berkeley Poets Co-op occurred in front of Cody's, at the corner of Telegraph and Haste, on a balmy Saturday afternoon in the spring of 1971. It was there that Co-op mainstay Bruce Hawkins caught my eye by flashing an early stapled edition of the Co-op's magazine at me as I waited for the traffic light to change. I had previously seen Bruce selling the magazine out of his knapsack on Telegraph and Shattuck Avenues in south Berkeley, and in front of Peet's coffee shop at Walnut Square, and the northside Co-op Market on Shattuck. I asked to see a copy and checked out one of his poems. Impressed, I gave Bruce a buck for the magazine and asked for more details about the Co-op. He told me it held a weekly workshop on Wednesday evenings where writers could read their poems and short prose and get feedback. They could also subsequently submit their finished work for possible publication in the semiannual Co-op magazine.

The idea of joining a writer's workshop appealed to me because I suspected that participating in one would motivate me to write more. Of course, it had to be the right kind of workshop, by which I meant one that was free of cliques. One that wasn't limited to an Academic or Beat ethos, that valued the development of one's craft and voice and a sense of revelation where, in James Dickey's memorable words, "A poet is someone who stands outside in the rain hoping to be struck by lightning."

Life Changes

The spring and summer of 1972 ushered in a number of momentous changes in my life. Disenchanted with textbook publishing, I resigned my editorial position with Wadsworth and bought a funky, 1965 Chevy pickup truck, with which I would, at least partially, support myself with a moving and hauling business over the next twenty years.

With the draft ended and the Vietnam War winding down, I was, in Timothy Leary's seductive mantra of the times, ready to "turn on, tune in and drop out." I wanted to decompress from the corporate world and pursue my literary interests. Like many of my Berkeley compatriots, I also wanted, if possible, to liberate myself from the shackles of my past conditioning. Toward this end, some of us explored body work in the form of Reichian therapy, bio-energetics, tai chi, and yoga, all of which shared an emphasis on paying close attention to one's breathing. We also steeped ourselves in the metaphysical works of Hermann Hesse (*Steppenwolf, Siddhartha,* and *The Glass Bead Game*), Carlos Castaneda (*The Teachings of Don Juan*), Aldous Huxley (*The Doors of Perception*) and Erich Neumann (*The Origin and History of Consciousness*). And we variously experimented with LSD, peyote, and psilocybin as a means of intensifying our awareness of everyday reality. Some of us were also drawn to more esoteric disciplines, such as creating, then meditating on, one's astrological chart, reading tarot cards, or throwing the *I Ching,* each of these practices serving as heuristic devices for externalizing and working with various dimensions of one's personality, as best described in Ralph Metzner's *Maps of Consciousness.*

The Berkeley Poets Co-op was a part of the social experimentation of the times. It was a democratically-inclined community of writers determined to act on KSAN radioman Scoop Nisker's challenge, "If you don't like the news, go out and make some of your own." The Co-op was sustained by Charles Entrekin, a poet, novelist, and cultural refugee from Birmingham, Alabama, with a highly developed sense of Southern hospitality. Charles, his son Demian, and his artist wife Maggie lived in a brown shingle house on Oregon Street in south Berkeley, where they hosted the weekly Co-op meetings downstairs. I soon became a regular at workshop meetings, which typically drew between ten and twenty writers, more or less evenly divided between men and women.

In many ways, the Co-op, from the summer of 1972 through the winter of 1975, became the fulcrum point from which my life radiated. Besides commenting on each other's writing, some of us regularly played pickup basketball games at the elementary school playground across the street from the Entrekin household. In the heat of the moment, the games occasionally got physically aggressive. A not-so-subtle elbow to the ribs sometimes served as a delayed rejoinder to prior Workshop criticism. Typically, Charles, Bruce Hawkins, Belden Johnson, Bruce Boston, Clive Matson, and I were joined by neighborhood walk-ons to complete the teams. Afterwards, we would cool off with a beer or two and enjoy a smoke as we caught our breath. Those were the days when smoking tobacco in public was still socially acceptable, a time when the basic writer's kit consisted of a blank page, a typewriter, a cup of coffee, and a cigarette.

I soon developed a close friendship outside the Workshop with Bruce and Anne Hawkins. This was during the summer of 1972, when Bobby Fischer and chess were all the rage in Berkeley and Telegraph Avenue cafés were filled with people playing (tick-tock) speed chess. More or less evenly matched, Bruce and I hung out at his duplex on Hopkins and played a number of leisurely games while Fischer defeated Boris Spassky at a hotel in Reykjavik, Iceland, and became the first and only American World Champion. After twenty-four years of Russian domination, the press jubilantly treated Fischer's demolition of Spassky as a Cold War victory for the USA.

When our interest in chess waned, our conversations moved to politics and Bruce's belief that population totals for various nation-states were routinely exaggerated by their bureaucracies, so as to make them appear far larger than they actually were. Lying about its demography, in Bruce's view, had become an integral part of the way a modern state obtains its funding, which is typically doled out on a *per capita* basis, a statistical game where the larger the population claimed, the more money a government gets to pay for its foreign and domestic expenses.

In the fall of 1973, Bruce and I collaborated on a broadcast at KPFA of my story "Depression Man." I narrated the basic text, while Bruce, with his rich baritone voice, dubbed in the newspaper headlines, television commercials, traffic, and weather reports that are interspersed throughout the story. KPFA, Berkeley's version of Radio Free America, was a strong supporter of regional writing and broadcast the work of a number of Co-op writers, especially on Denny Smithson's morning program.

I had written a number of poems since joining the Co-op and decided to publish them as a twenty-eight page chapbook entitled *The Familiar Stranger*. Anne Hawkins drew and designed the cover, and Maggie Entrekin provided a pen-and-ink portrait. My plan was to print a thousand copies at a unit cost of thirty cents and, hopefully, to hawk them on the street for a buck apiece.

Through a process of trial and error, I learned that three hours, give or take fifteen minutes, was normally all the time I needed to sell a dozen or so copies of *The Familiar Stranger*. Whenever I tried putting in more than three hours or worked more than three straight days, I discovered that my enthusiasm for street sales waned.

Because I had gotten used to reading my poems aloud at the Co-op Workshop, I found it relatively easy to ask potential buyers of my chapbook if they would like to hear a short poem or two. If they expressed interest I would recite "Humanity" and/or "Gross National Product" as pithy examples of my work:

HUMANITY

Sometimes I don't want
To relate to anybody or anything
But myself
(So I can check out the damage).

When I'm like this
I feel agitated
And your vibrations hurt
My jangled nerve ends.

If you touch me now
I'll close up
Like a snail.

GROSS NATIONAL PRODUCT

A Drunk
Has gotten into the cab
Behind the wheel of a loaded truck
Taken ten Dexedrine   and is on
The road   out of control
If you ask him to slow down
He won't hear
He's liable to kill you
Because he doesn't know
How to
STOP

More often than not, reading either one or both of these poems helped me close the sale. In working the cafés, it became apparent that nearly half of the people who bought a copy of *The Familiar Stranger* did so because they were tourists happy to get an inexpensive memento from "Berzerkeley." For a buck, how could they go wrong?

Living Cheaply in Berkeley

Looking back on my stint as a street seller, I have to pinch myself when recalling how cheap it was to live in the southern and western flatlands of Berkeley in the early 1970s. I could actually live well on three hundred fifty a month, or twelve dollars a day. My rent, phone and utilities, now shared with a roommate, came to less than two dollars a day. Since I could walk to anywhere in south Berkeley within twenty minutes, I saved on gas and parking by not having to drive my pickup. Food and drink on Telegraph was not only inexpensive, but also varied and delicious. On mornings when I felt like eating breakfast out, I would stroll up to Telegraph and Dwight to Bongo Burgers and order their ninety-nine-cent special, which consisted of two eggs, hash browns, toast, and coffee. Or I might amble over to the Caffé Med and buy black coffee and a scone for a dollar and then grab a table with an abandoned *Chronicle* on it, so I could read the latest box scores and catch up on how the Oakland A's were doing. For lunch or dinner, I sometimes moseyed up to Kip's on Durant and, for a buck-and-a-half, purchased one of their cheeseburgers, which came with a generous salad bar. Or I might return to Bongo Burgers and devour a falafel or Louleh Kebab with a Pepsi for less than two dollars. After catching a foreign flick at the Pacific Film Archive, I often stopped for a late-evening snack at Top Dog and ordered a tasty Kielbasa sausage smothered with onions, ketchup, and sauerkraut.

The Pacific Film Archive was a Mecca for foreign film buffs. For a buck a film, one could take in the (mostly subtitled) work of the great foreign directors. The PFA is where I was first exposed to such classic films as Ingmar Bergman's *The Seventh Seal, Wild Strawberries, The Virgin Spring, Cries & Whispers* and *The Magic Flute,* which featured such great actors as Max von Sydow and Liv Ullmann. Or Akira Kurosawa's *Seven Samurai, Yojimbo, Rashomon* and *Red Beard,* starring the inimitable Toshiro Mifune. Or Federico Fellini's *La Dolce Vita, Divorce Italian Style, 8 ½,* and *Satyricon,* which showcased the work of Marcello Mastroianni, Sophia Loren and Anouk Aimée. From behind the Iron Curtain, the illuminating early work of Polish director Roman Polanski (*Knife in the Water*) and Czech directors Milos Forman (*The Firemen's Ball*), Jan Nemec (*Diamonds of the Night*) and Jiri Menzel (*Closely Watched Trains*) were but some of the films that captured my imagination.

Another component of living cheaply but well in the 1970s revolved around Moe's Books and his innovative cash or trade policy. One could go into Moe's with a bag of used books and get enough trade credit to pay for a whole new round of purchases. The way it worked was this: Moe would offer fifty percent more in trade credit than he would pay out in cash. If you didn't get cash, you got a green credit slip with a picture of Moe on the front side and the amount of trade credit written on the back. Moe's Money, as the green slips came to be known, then became a kind of legal tender for the purchase of used books within the confines of the store. When you needed cash, you could also sell your trade slips to other Moe's customers at a discounted price. Trading their used books for Moe's Money was not only a good deal for customers, it was also a shrewd way for Moe to greatly increase his inventory without having to tie up a lot of cash. Since there was always a fresh batch of used books coming in, I made it a point to check the shelves several times a week to see, for example, if a copy of Ezra Pound's *Cantos* or a novel by Milan Kundera had arrived.

City Miner

During the fall and winter of 1975, I mulled over the idea of starting a quarterly magazine that would reflect and celebrate the rich, but neglected, veins of cultural creativity that permeated the Bay Area and northern California. By January of 1976, I decided, with Bruce Boston's encouragement and editorial support, to take the plunge and publish the first issue of *City Miner* in the Spring. I "invested" the last $1,500 of my savings to cover the cost of the initial 3,000-copy print run, with the hope that I could sell enough copies (along with some display ads) to pay for the second issue. The Berkeley Poets Co-op was no longer the primary focus of my attention, but I kept in touch with a number of its members, whose poems, short stories, and essays appeared in *City Miner* over the years.

And so it went. My life in Berkeley an ongoing experiment, with one thing serendipitously leading to the next. Where everything is connected, though not necessarily in the manner we expect. So goodbye and thanks to the Berkeley Poets Co-op, hello to *City Miner* magazine and City Miner Books. Hats off to John Raeside and the *Eastbay Express* and to Peter Berg and *Planet Drum*. To all the good stories yet to be told.

SALES

Charles Entrekin

Initially, we decided that Co-op members would be responsible for selling at least 50 copies of each issue and that they would get 50 percent of their sales. Eventually, however, some poets discovered they could supplement their personal incomes by selling the *Berkeley Poets Cooperative* on the streets. As time passed and production quality increased, a few, like Bruce Hawkins, became quite successful, were recognized on the streets, and began to bring in some real money. So Bruce and a few others took over the major work of sales. You can see a photo of Bruce on the streets of Berkeley in the cover story in the August 29, 1976, issue of *The New York Times Magazine*. One of our members, an attractive young woman, Judith Stone, would dress up— artistic scarf, sexy skirt, black knit stockings, wide-brimmed hat and veil, high-heel shoes, and heavy makeup—and stand in front of what was then the Shattuck Avenue Co-op grocery store. She would sell out all of her 50 copies in just a few hours.

The sales from each issue were used to finance the next issue. We were fiscally sound, actually making enough money to do some marketing, and we were providing a few poets with some real financial help.

Publishing two or more issues a year, we successfully sold out every issue. Over the years, we continued to increase our press run, from 500 up to around 2,500, but we kept our prices low. We priced the *Berkeley Poets Cooperative* magazine for local Berkeley street sales, not for distributors or bookstores. Bookstores and distributors were nice, but our focus and our best and most important audience continued to be local Berkeley students and citizens. To accommodate local sales, we lowered the price in 1971 to $1.00 for Issue #3. Each time we adjusted the price on the magazine, we had a discussion about what people on the street would be willing to pay. In our cost-benefit analysis, we tried to weigh the street-market value against the income received by the Co-op and the poets selling the magazine. Holding the price low was a premium, but every few years we had to reevaluate the market. In 1974, Issue #5 was $1.25. Two years later, with Issue #10, we bumped the price to $1.50. And by 1982, six years later, we raised it to $3.00 for Issue #20. Our next-to-last Issue #29 was still only $5.00 in 1987.

We had built a reputation on the affordability and quality of the work with our readers in the Bay Area. If we were late with a new issue, our "regulars" began asking for it. And Bruce Hawkins would tell us to get busy with the next issue because, well, he needed the money and, as Peter Dreyer in *San Francisco Magazine* said, "The Berkeley Poets Cooperative publishes some of the most accomplished work I have thus far come across in my efforts to define what is being done, and not being done, in Bay Area poetry."

BPC Years: 1970–1988

A STRING OF BEGINNINGS

Bruce Hawkins

I probably came to the Co-op with lower expectations than most of the people I later invited to the open readings.

We all, I think, were asked as children what we wanted to be when we grew up, and as long as we could say "fireman" or "the president" or many of the other chestnuts, it was cool. And if we later could say "accountant" or "lawyer," it was even cooler. But then, some of us would say "poet" and the well-meaning, in-our-own-best-interest advice set in: "In this society, poets just don't earn a living."

Many, many years, many, many jobs had passed, and I had hit a fairly desperate stage. My ridiculous, inexorable logic told me, "If poets don't earn a living, poets are, by definition, disabled." I went to the welfare department and demanded they publish my book as a rehabilitation project. Mere theater! Expecting nothing! It was one of a string of dumb things I did. They, of course, said, "No."

But it happened that one of the original Co-op members was a social worker there. He told someone to tell me about the Poets Cooperative, which had self-published a magazine and had readings every Wednesday night.

So I came to Oregon Street. It must have been summer 1970; it was still daylight. I went upstairs to the small front room. It wasn't an attic but seemed like one. The window looked out over the basketball courts across the street. I liked it!

There were six people there: Charles and Maggie Entrekin, Ted Fleischman, Rod Tulloss, Bruce Boston, and Rona Spalten. Since Maggie didn't write, Rona was the only woman poet. That was the main weakness early on. I think Judy Stone already lived downstairs, but she was Maggie's friend and felt diffident about joining the guys. I must say here, my memory is full of holes. I cultivate it that way, so if any of you who were there cry, "Wrong, wrong," I acquiesce. The first issue contained six male poets and Maggie's art work. The guys were: two social workers (who showed up only for parties), two programmers (Charles and Bruce), a mathematician (Rod), and a physicist (Ted). Rod was still in the doctoral program at Cal, and I don't think Ted actually worked as a physicist. Rona's husband, Jack, who wasn't there but occasionally showed up to listen, was Gonzo tech, the kind of guy who could stand around at a party with a drink in his hand watching chip structures float by in his head.

I'm getting ahead of myself, but this original make-up of the Co-op was important in terms of criticism. It was never, "Right on, brother," which had been my fear going in; it was analytical without descending into literary *Jeopardy*, which is what often happened in a room full of English majors. I'd been in many workshops and was the closest thing the Co-op had to an English major for quite a while.

Someone read a poem. We talked. Someone read. We talked, and within a half hour I had my first first: I would be coming back. After the first year and a half, my life blended into week after week of workshops and day after day on the street with my pack full of books. Most of the memories I have for those fifteen years are, at least peripherally, Co-op memories. It's way beyond the scope of this, or even a much longer this. So I'm limiting myself to a sequence of firsts.

If a poem read at a workshop is good, bad, or indifferent is a matter of indifference. What gets said afterward, and how, sets the tone. My "Right on!" fears were quickly banished. What I remember most from the first night is the criticism/commentary of Rod Tulloss, and I remember no word of it, just the very good sense. And the very pleasant room Charles and Maggie provided.

I became a regular. A few new people arrived: Lucy Day, Kathleen Raven. The elephant in the room was about a hundred unsold copies of the first issue with no obvious way to unload them. The friend-and-relative purchases had been made.

There was a KPFA fair in a big, white church/hall (was it Finnish?) below San Pablo, and we decided to give it a try. We sold 50 copies in a couple of hours. I think I sold 30. That was my first taste of selling, and it sold me. I would self-publish *Less Power* and try selling Co-op magazines, if we could find a way to publish Issue #2.

There was a Taxi Unlimited party at Virginia and McGee where I met Clive Matson. I don't know the exact sequence of it. I told him about the Co-op. He came to the readings. He had a letter press in his attic on lower Hearst Street. He said he'd print an issue as a kind of apprenticeship if we'd all pitch in. All we needed was paper. I think we paid for that, although someone might have lifted it from work. If we did chip in for it, it was our last touch of vanity press. After that, sales paid for the magazine and eventually grants covered the Chapbook Series.

I'm on the street, on Durant above Telegraph, right below the steps that come down from what was then the women's softball field, in the present tense, because it is so gut-wrenching. Students are flowing past, frat guys: "I hate poetry," "Get that outta my face."

I'm about to quit. The KPFA fair was a setup. Even if someone at KPFA *hated* poetry, they wouldn't say it in that environment.

The hourly rush of class change has just passed by. The empty street with no sales in sight is still better than all the rejection I've had to stomach. It seems like I've been out for hours without a sale. I haven't. Quite.

A girl comes, walking slowly, no class to get to. She stops, she looks, she smiles, she buys. I stick a buck in my pocket. I'm in business. Back to the past tense. I may have been within five minutes of packing it in. That's how it felt. My basic stubbornness would most likely have prevailed even without the sale.

Now comes the last major first. This will be a hard one for me to write: I have to deal with poetic quality and the nature of our Cooperative. I'd gotten used to the street. I'd sold *Less Power* and Co-op #2. Co-op #3 was either out or in progress. I was giving everyone who would stop long enough to listen the Oregon Street address.

We moved to the big room downstairs, may have occasionally had more than 25 people. Many would show up and leave because they couldn't get a chance to read.

Local poets who were or who considered themselves successful wouldn't be caught dead at our workshops. We were still thought of as at-least-borderline vanity press. As a cooperative, we were committed to publishing something by everyone who participated in the workshops and who submitted. To enhance quality, we encouraged large submissions. If not quality, it gave us choice.

We published some poets whose work we didn't like. Whether it was bad is a subjective call. It wasn't the kind of poetry that some people hate—we prided ourselves on publishing that. Mildly desperate blandness, well-mannered docility is the best way I can characterize it. It gave a feel that we would publish things that no magazine with a critical editorial staff would touch, things with a trail of hundreds of well-deserved rejection slips dragging behind them, and things that couldn't be called surreal or experimental in any way. And how do you say, "Get that shit out of here," to the most polite, alert workshop attendee you could imagine? Bruce Boston often played "bad cop"—he was the only one up to it.

This was a problem at the time for everyone, but I felt particularly guilty because I was the one wandering the streets handing out blanket invitations. Was our cooperative commitment going to drag us down? Age was a factor. Young poets who don't fit in and who choose not to leave can usually change their style; but people my age at the time (mid-thirties) or older tend, as writers, to be what they are. Period. So we had docility bred with a bulldog. Remember, we were just coming out of the era when you couldn't trust anyone over thirty.

So it was Wednesday. About twenty people in the room ready to read. A woman, about my age, sat across from me, very quiet, a little nervous. She made a "Can-I-read-one?" motion. And it was Alicia Ostriker. She blew us all away.

That was the first time I felt justified and confident I could tell everyone who would listen that we had open readings every Wednesday, with no fear I was dragging the group down.

The Co-op was rolling. Then Charles went to Montana for a year, and we had to leave the womb, find other, many other, living rooms. One of the places, Marina's apartment on Allston Way, turned out to be one of my previous Berkeley homes. There were probably more than twenty of those by then. Kelsey Street Press emerged from that time.

Charles came back. Picnics, parties (Betsy and I throwing things at each other), basketball, softball, chess, The New York Times. We were an institution. We produced an anthology of work from 1970-1980. Alicia, back in New Jersey, along with Rod, who had moved there, started a sister magazine, U.S. 1. They also did an anthology. Mike Helm started City Miner Magazine.

About the time of our 30th issue, I turned fifty. When selling, I started to feel like a relic, wandering around among the children of hippies who were more likely to be born-agains than Ginsbergers (*peyote in a bun*).

Starting with WordStar and the goal of printing out perfect copies of my poems on the clattering daisywheels at Berkeley's Vista College, I realized I'd been working with databases since I discovered the *Baseball Guide* at the age of nine, and ended up using computers well enough to disappear into the world of work.

The Co-op continued. Charles and Gail Entrekin kept my poems in circulation and got me published in more magazines than I had been able to myself.

1973

Contributors: Marcia Falk, Alicia Ostriker, Dennis Anderson, Michael Helm, Lucille Day, Clive Matson, Susan Stern, Judith Stone, Dan Balderston, Aaron Poller, Jennifer Stone, Peri Danton, Marina deBellagente Bostedt, Scott Lowell, Rodham Elliott Tulloss, Charles Klein, Patricia Dienstfrey, Jim Tinen, Karen Brodine, Ted Fleischman, Bruce Hawkins, Rosemary Christoph, Margaret Teague, Charles Entrekin, Bruce Boston, Rona Spalten, Jennifer Bramhall, Maggie Entrekin.

Cover & layout: Gary Head

BPC Years: 1970–1988

WASN'T THAT A TIME?

Anne Hawkins

I became an associate member of the Poets Co-op soon after
my husband, Bruce, went to a meeting in 1970. I'm sure the term
"associate member" didn't exist yet; the whole endeavor was new and
fluid. One of the things we liked immediately about the group was its
do-it-yourself attitude toward publishing, born partly from philosophy
and partly from necessity.

Clive Matson has a press? Great; he can print Issue #2. Anne
Hawkins, as well as Maggie Entrekin, is an artist? Maggie did Issue
#1, so Anne can do the cover of Issue #2. (This was a mistake. I drew,
painted, and etched, but knew nothing about graphic design until
much later. Fortunately, it didn't seem to hurt sales!)

As word spread, more and more poets, prose writers and just
curious people came to meetings. I remember setting up many folding
chairs at the Entrekins' Oregon Street house and returning later to
find standing room only. In 1970, the '60s mentality of communal
activity continued to thrive. Small cooperatives and collectives, such
as Taxi Unlimited and The Cheese Board Collective, flourished. The
Vietnam War raged on, and Berkeley had recently been through the
trauma of People's Park. After our son, David, had to shelter-in-place
at Washington Elementary as gas from helicopters rained down (we
had marched and protested with the rest), we chose to move to North
Berkeley, what we called the Far North. Now, with the Poets Co-op,
we were back in our old south Berkeley haunts. We'd found, not only
a good literary home-base for Bruce, but a comfortable ambience and
potential good friends.

Over the years I contributed art, mine and others, for issues of
the magazine. Tony Dubovsky provided excellent covers that gave the
magazine a clean, professional look. Bruce published poems and sold
out issue after issue of 2,000 copies. (Of course, not *all* sold by him!)
Eventually I studied typography and design, created a logo for the
press, did the book and cover design for Bruce's chapbook *The Ghost of*

the Buick and the book design for Lucy (Lucille) Day's *Self-Portrait with Hand Microscope*.

These pieces came in handy when I applied for a publications job at Cal's Center for Slavic and East European Studies. I'd more or less forgiven UC Berkeley for People's Park; after all, Bruce and I had met on campus. In fact, we first published together in Cal's literary magazine, *The Occident*; one of my drawings was of him playing the recorder—naked, though that didn't show. I'd also done some undergraduate work and gotten my M.A. there.

At the Slavic Center, I solicited articles and interviewed faculty and grad students for a quarterly newsletter, did book design and production, etc. All those years of hanging around writers finally paid off! I worked there through the Gorbachev years and the demise of the USSR—a very exciting period to be thrown into an area of scholarship about which I knew little at first.

Bruce, meanwhile, learned to program and landed a position at the district office of Peralta Community Colleges, doing work that engaged him, though (as was true for me, too) making it nearly impossible to do his own work. Charles helped along the way, hiring him for a time at his then-company, The Application Group. Thanks so much, Charles. Bruce retired in 2009.

Once in a while I'll walk through a room and realize I haven't tripped over a single cardboard box of shrink-wrapped magazines or chapbooks. It still feels strange. We remember so many friends and places over so many years, it's impossible to do them justice. We sat around our kitchen table, Mike's, Charles's; we enjoyed many, many readings at Cody's Books and other venues; we drank too much beer at Brennan's (the *real* Brennan's) afterward; and I watched countless Co-op softball and pickup basketball games. Chess was played as well, trips taken, parties thrown. Children were born and grew. Now Cody's is closed and greatly missed. The last Cody's event I remember us all attending was Gail Entrekin's 2005 reading from her powerful book, *Change (will do you good)*. For us, it was a terrific way to end (or not?) an era.

WHY THE BERKELEY POETS COOPERATIVE WAS SUCCESSFUL

Bruce Boston

What does it mean to be a successful small press publisher? The average small press literary magazine survives for one-and-a-half issues and about a year. The Berkeley Poets Cooperative survived as an active group for more than two decades. It published thirty issues of its magazine, 28 books by individual writers, and a best-of anthology spanning the years 1970–1980. At its peak, the magazine was selling more than 1,500 copies per issue. And many of the chapbooks also sold well. BPC was clearly a resounding success by small press standards.

I joined the Berkeley Poets Cooperative in 1970, shortly after the first issue of the magazine was published, and was an active member for most of the next twenty years. At different times, I served on editorial staffs, successfully applied for a local grant, handled mail-order distribution, did layout, worked with printers, sold the magazine on the streets of Berkeley, etc. The workshops helped me hone and polish my craft as a poet and writer. Being involved in the editing and production of the magazine and the business side of BPC proved to be an extensive lesson in small press publishing, as it existed at the time.

Apart from some outstanding poems and stories, and the satisfaction of finding an outlet for my own poetry and fiction, what I remember most about the experience are the people who passed through the BPC during its existence: the camaraderie and the conflicts, the friendships, love affairs, and enmities. In the early years, when the spirit of the late sixties was still alive and the workshops were located close to Telegraph Avenue, all kinds of poets and would-be poets passed through, all shapes and sizes and ages, from teenage runaways to widely published and established authors. Many returned to stay for years as I did, and became involved not only in the workshops, but in the publication of the magazine. And as I did, they all contributed in varying degrees to the accomplishments of the BPC.

Yet of all these individuals, two stand out in my mind as the mainstays of the group, and as being most responsible for its longevity and success: Charles Entrekin and Bruce Hawkins.

Charles was the *paterfamilias* of the group from the beginning. Over the years, most of the workshops and business meetings took place at his house. But far more than providing a physical locale for the group, Charles set the right tone for both its workshops and its activities as a press. I'd been in other writing workshops prior to BPC, but none proved as valuable for me. Most of the ones I attended I felt were too supportive, praising mediocre work so as not to hurt anyone's feelings, and thus worthless in terms of teaching anyone how to improve their writing. I was in a fiction workshop at the University of California that did take a more critical stance, but the professor seemed so bored with teaching the class that it lacked any vitality. None of these writing workshops achieved the tone that Charles set, combining a supportive response with criticism, and always showing a genuine interest in the poems that were read. Charles is a fine poet, but that is no guarantee of skill in leading a writing workshop. I don't know if his approach came naturally to him, or if he learned it from some former mentor from his own educational background. Whatever, the result was a workshop that continued to draw members week after week and year after year, and was a success in teaching those who attended how to write better poetry.

At the level of managing a small press, Charles also met the task, not merely with the decisions he made, but in his management of people. Anyone who has ever worked in any kind of organization knows the personal conflicts that can arise and how destructive they can be. Volunteer organizations such as BPC are no exception to this rule. Charles demonstrated a talent for smoothing over the waters in such instances, creating a compromise that left the conflicting participants if not happy, at least satisfied with the result. I credit his ability on this count to his Southern charm and natural savvy.

So the workshops were first rate. The business of publishing an attractive magazine and books filled with quality poetry and fiction worked well. But what good are such publications if no one buys them? This is where Bruce Hawkins entered the equation. I believe Bruce joined BPC the same year I did. From his readings in the workshop, it was immediately clear that he was an outstanding poet. His comments and criticism in the workshops were also a plus. But these were not his main contribution to the group.

Most of the members of BPC tried at one time or another to sell the magazine on the streets of Berkeley. Some had very little success or, like me, only marginal success for the time put in. Others discovered they could sell quite well, but soon became bored with the process. Bruce Hawkins proved himself to be the exception. Day after day, week after week, through fair weather and foul, through encounters with the Berkeley Police who, oblivious to the First Amendment and freedom of the press, thought you needed a license to sell publications on the street, he persevered. For many years he sold the majority of the copies of each issue on the streets of Berkeley, thus generating most of the revenue that kept the press solvent.

I'm not positive why Hawkins was so successful at selling the magazine. With his shaggy hair and beard and gold-rimmed glasses, he looked more the part of a poet than most, and that may have helped. He certainly never applied high-pressure sales tactics. Instead, he seemed to radiate a kind of modest yet assured confidence, perhaps even an indifference as to whether someone purchased the magazine or not. He almost seemed to be saying: "This is a good publication that is well worth reading. It's your loss if you pass it by."

Thanks to all who made BPC not only a success over the years, but one of the more rewarding and memorable experiences of my life as a writer, with a generous nod to the roles that Charles Entrekin and Bruce Hawkins played. Hope we can do it again someday, next time around on the wheel.

Number 7

Berkeley Poets Cooperative

1974

Contributors: Belden Johnson, Betsy Huebner, Marina deBellegente Bostedt, Richard Strong, Michael Helm, Alicia Ostriker, Karen Brodine, Lucille Day, Dino Siotis, Nina Rogozen, Kate Rose, Charles Entrekin, Ted Fleischman, Edgar Austin, Patricia Dienstfrey, Quinton Duval, Bruce Hawkins, James Tinen, Laurel Taylor, Daniel Balderston, John Allen Cann, Kara Schmidt, Bruce Boston, Laura Moriarty, Kit Duane, Rod Tulloss, Jennifer Stone, Richard Tokeshi, Paul Aebersold, James Barker, Loughran O'Connor.

Cover: Russ Leong
Layout: Gary Head
Staff: Belden Johnson, Karen Brodine, Lucille Day, Laura Moriarty, Susan Stern, James Tinen

BPC Years: 1971–1982

TO BE A POET

Lucille Lang Day

The first time I heard about the Berkeley Poets Co-op was when my friend Paul Aebersold showed me a set of colorful posters he'd made by silk-screening his photographs and pairing them with quotes from poems by Co-op members. It was the fall of 1971, and I was twenty-three years old.

Although I was a graduate student in zoology, the idea of the Co-op intrigued me because I had aspired to be a poet since childhood. I began to think of myself as a poet after writing my first poem at age six. When I showed it to my first-grade teacher, Miss Clydesdale, however, I was sorry, because she asked me to read it to the class. Too shy to do so, I looked down and mumbled. It would be another twenty years before I could enjoy giving a poetry reading.

In fifth grade, my desire to be a poet intensified when I encountered Emily Dickinson's poem "Success." I was enthralled by "To comprehend a nectar/requires sorest need." Anticipating adulthood, I knew I would not always get what I wanted, and this was a fabulous way of expressing that. I wanted to write like that too, but I knew that my own poems were only those of a child. I was eager to grow up and write real poems, and I did not think I would need any special study or training to do it. I thought it would just happen when I grew up.

As an undergraduate at UC Berkeley, I decided to major in science although I also still wanted to be a poet. I now wanted to be both a scientist and a writer, and no one had told me these were both full-time jobs. Emily Dickinson and Madame Curie were my heroines. I thought that by studying science I could maximize my contribution to society, increase my employability, and have another whole realm of knowledge to bring to my writing.

I didn't find much time to write during my college years, but in the spring of my senior year, 1971, my muse woke up. I wrote a lot of poems and submitted some to contests for Berkeley students.

As a biology major who'd taken three literature classes, I knew I was at a disadvantage, but I hoped nevertheless that I might win something.

I received Honorable Mention for a group of seven rhymed poems I submitted to the Dorothy Rosenberg Memorial Prize competition in Lyric Poetry. The congratulatory letter I received from the chair of the prize committee said that Professor Harder, who had judged the contest, wrote, "The author of manuscript 208 should be given Honorable Mention for his/her sensitive treatment of several topical themes. I am sorry there is no second prize." I came in second against the undergraduate and graduate English majors! I took this as a sign that I was a true poet. I now realize that the poems I sent to the Dorothy Rosenberg contest were juvenilia, but at the time I didn't even know what juvenilia was.

Paul decided to sell the communal house he owned and ran in Oakland. His real estate agent, Kathleen Raven, was a member of the Berkeley Poets Co-op, and she and Paul held a party on April 1, 1972, to celebrate the sale of the house. It was my opportunity to meet the Co-op members.

As I leaned against a doorpost and tapped my foot in time to the music, Ted Fleischman, one of the Co-op cofounders, said, "You look like you want to dance."

We danced, we dated, we shared our poetry, and by summer we were living together. All spring and summer I pleaded with Ted to take me to a Berkeley Poets Co-op meeting, but he said they already had enough people and advised me to start my own group. I would later learn that Co-op meetings were open to anyone who wanted to attend. I think he didn't want to take me because he didn't think my poems were very good and didn't think the other Co-op members would, either. Finally, in August, he said they didn't have so many people now and it was a good time to join.

The Co-op was then meeting in the living room of Charles and Maggie Entrekin's house on Oregon Street in Berkeley. At my first meeting, I decided to read a couple of my Honorable Mention poems, although I considered them finished poems, because I thought they were my best poems and I wanted to make a good impression. When I looked up at the faces around me as I read the opening lines of, "I Hear

Them" ("I hear them/As they make the fields ring./At six. a.m./Outside my pane they sing"), I knew I was in trouble. After a few moments of stunned silence, the dozen or so poets present informed me that the poem was trite, boring, and predictable. I read another poem and received the same response.

Thinking maybe these weren't the best of my best poems, I went back the following week and read a couple more of my Honorable Mention poems, including one dedicated to Heisenberg and written from the point of view of an electron. It begins: "Is the magic probability/Four pi psi-quared, r-squared dee r?/Do you really think you'll catch me/Near the atom's crackling star?" This time, the Co-op members lost their patience with me. One man summed up the feeling in the room as he said with exasperation: "We told you last week to stop writing this stuff!"

This did not deter me from going back. I took it as a challenge to write a good unrhymed poem, something that the Co-op members would praise. To get inspired, I started reading several books of contemporary poetry every week (so much for my graduate work in zoology!). Up until then, my favorite poets had been Keats, Shelley, Dickinson, and Millay. Now I discovered that I liked Sylvia Plath, Anne Sexton, and William Carlos Williams just as well.

Every Wednesday night I took my latest efforts to the Co-op workshop. I was not completely satisfied with this work myself, so I was neither surprised nor offended when it was criticized. What really surprised me was that I found it hard to write unrhymed poetry that was any good. I knew my rhymed poems were not in the same league as those of Shelley or Keats, but I could excuse myself for not attaining the highest level in something that at least *looked* difficult. It was harder to excuse myself for not excelling at something that looked easy.

After I'd been attending the Co-op meetings for a few months, two other poets who wrote formal poems as well as free verse came on the scene: Marcia Falk and Dan Balderston. To my astonishment, Marcia's poem "Letter to the Sons of Abraham," written in rhyming quatrains in iambic pentameter, and Dan's sonnet "To Emily Dickinson" practically received standing ovations. So the Co-op members weren't totally opposed to rhymed poems! I asked Charles

Entrekin why people liked Marcia's and Dan's rhymed poems but not mine. He said, "Because theirs use contemporary language and deal with contemporary issues."

I enjoyed presenting my poems at the Co-op, hearing poems by other poets, hearing critiques of the other poems, and also responding to poems myself. I discovered that even as one of the least experienced members of a literary workshop, I could always find something to say. This was in sharp contrast to my behavior in science seminars, where I was as mute as the chairs, feeling more like an observer than a participant in the goings-on. I began to realize that I was more a writer than a scientist, and that in a literary milieu my greatest inspiration and strongest opinions would surface.

Alas, however, writing a good poem was no easy matter, and it was about a year before I could write a halfway decent poem with any reliability. It felt like a breakthrough in July 1973 when I wrote a poem called "The Lab," whose opening lines are "My snails caress/the planetary stillness,/dropping opaque eggs/to settle among the elements." It was a poem about being uncomfortable in the laboratory: my shortcomings as a scientist had led to one of my first real poems.

I attended the Co-op workshop pretty regularly for four years, but in 1976 I decided I wanted feedback on my work from a wider range of writers. That summer I went to the Squaw Valley Community of Writers, and in the fall I took a poetry workshop with Josephine Miles at Berkeley. In the years to come, I would return twice to the Squaw Valley Community of Writers and eventually earn an M.A. in English and an M.F.A. in creative writing at San Francisco State University.

In 1982 Robert Pinsky, David Littlejohn, and Michael Rubin selected my first poetry collection, *Self-Portrait with Hand Microscope*, for the Joseph Henry Jackson Award from San Francisco Foundation. Berkeley Poets Workshop and Press published the book later that year.

I now write mostly free verse, but occasionally a sonnet or villanelle will arrive at the door to my brain and demand to be let in. This is a sonnet from *The Curvature of Blue* (Cervena Barva, 2009):

DESCRIBING THE MONARCHS
For Richard

"Too bad that 'bloom' is overused," you say
as we stand beneath a eucalyptus tree,
your arm around me, head bent back to see
the monarchs celebrating New Year's Day.
"And 'burn' is wrong, and 'rust' suggests decay,
but I like 'bless.'" A thousand blessings cling,
each with white spots on black-and-orange wings,
to branches unaccustomed to such beauty.

But burn they do: each tiny, beating flame
lights up the tree, a bloom that's made of fire,
flickering in winter to proclaim
a leaf gives solace, milkweed sates desire.
They smolder, cool as rust, in spangled air,
then fly like sparks, illumining the year.

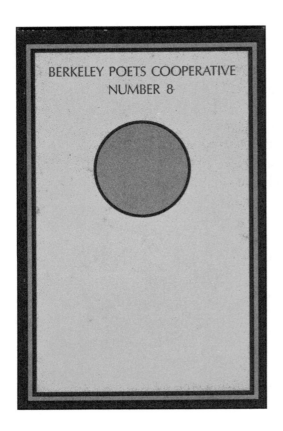

BERKELEY POETS COOPERATIVE
NUMBER 8

1974

Contributors: Kathleen Raven, Belden Johnson, Laura Schiff, Alan Bern, Edward Sause, Rena Rosenwasser, Terry Lauher, Roswell Spafford, Kate Rose, Peter Holland, Sandra Corrie Newmann, Mary Reutzinger, Richard Strong, Marcia Falk, Marina LaPalma, John Yurechko, Milo Miles, Alica Ostriker, Lucille Day, Clive Matson, John Wittmayer, Laura Moriarty, Nina Rogozen, John Allen Cann, Patricia Dienstfrey, Karen Brodine, Lorre Sintetos, Jennifer Stone, Paul Bendix, Shane Weare, Celeste Ericksson, Sally Weare.

Cover: Betsy Huebner
Layout: Ted Fleischman
Art Consultant: Anne Hawkins

THE LONG REACH OF THE BPC

Alicia Ostriker

It could be the best advice, as a poet, I ever had in my life. My family was about to spend the spring semester of 1972 in Berkeley, and my Princeton poet-acquaintance Rod Tulloss, who had been there, suggested I get in touch with his friend Charles Entrekin and find out about the Berkeley Poets Co-op. So I did, and so I came to sit on the floor, or a cushion, or a sagging couch, along with a mixed batch of other poets.

I loved Berkeley. My husband was on leave from Princeton University as a visiting lecturer in the Berkeley Astrophysics Department. I was on leave from Rutgers University doing research on William Blake. Our daughters were in first and second grade, and we had an au pair girl from Norway living with us to mind our two-year-old son, in a cramped apartment on McKinley Avenue. I had posters of Indian deities on the wall and Indian spreads on the beds; Jerry had a Honda 350 motorcycle and I had my bike to get around on. I think we were, maybe a little weirdly, trying to re-live our student days. Certainly we were glad to be away—New Yorkers by birth and upbringing that we were—from the bubble of social unreality that was Princeton. Princeton was pretty— everyone would say, "Oh you're so lucky to be living in Princeton, it's so pretty." Berkeley wasn't pretty at all. Not our part of it. Berkeley was alive. It was a mix of chic and raggedy that I could understand and enjoy, it had great bookstores and coffee shops, it had People's Park and the fascinating cast of characters on Telegraph Avenue. The junkies didn't distress me the way they distressed some people. Seemed to me, if they were going to exist, they might as well be out on the street where they could keep each other company. I liked watching Julia Vinograd—the Bubble Lady— walking up and down blowing iridescent bubbles from a kid's little plastic bottle—bubbles as charming as her poems were sharp and full of heart. Then there was Jack Micheline walking up and down looking like a bum, shouting his poems and hawking them for a buck. I'd met Jack in New York, when he was slightly less down on his luck. I was embarrassed at the way he was making a fool of himself—until at some point I realized, no, I was wrong and Jack was right. If you want to be a poet you *have* to be willing to make a fool of yourself.

Before becoming a regular at Berkeley Poets Cooperative, I tried sitting in on Josephine Miles' poetry workshops. Professor Miles's was famous as a poet-critic who wrote in a poker-face witty manner that I admired, and was equally famous for not letting disability (crippling arthritis) cramp her vitality. I'd heard her workshops were wonderful. Probably they were wonderful, but not for me. For me they were too tidy and too top-down. Twenty or so students sat in a neat circle, more or less at her feet, read their poems, and listened to her comments on them. Her comments were smart and insightful, but...they were only hers. And the poems were competent but cautious.

At Charles's house there was wine. People sat and slouched around randomly. Charles was benign and apparently laid-back, his poetry was dedicated to telling truths, his Alabama accent bathed us in a kind of musical honey, yet he managed to keep this bunch of potential rowdies orderly. This wasn't an academic group. This was townies. People talked when they felt like talking. People disagreed. Nobody was cautious. Nobody was angling for status, or so it seemed to me (I was probably wrong). I was in awe of Bruce Hawkins' low-key humor, amused by Ted Fleischman, bothered by Belden Johnson, and instinctively felt I had common cause with the women. Oh, delicate Patricia Dienstfrey, rational Lucille Day, intense Karen Brodine, wonderfully incomprehensible Marina LaPalma, passionate Betsy Huebner, wicked mad Irishwoman Jennifer Stone, who once came to a party dressed in blue loony clothes with a blue sequin on her 45-year old cheek. We were free, and we excluded nobody. The night we went around a table communally and hilariously collating copies of the magazine was one of the happiest nights I can remember. I hadn't felt so at home ever in my life.

Then it was June, the semester was over, and I had to leave Berkeley. Filled with melancholy and self-pity, feeling as if it was all just a dream and would be washed away like a window washed with rain. Goodbye little house. Bed on the floor, goodbye. Goodbye Sather Gate morning crowds; vendors setting up; Bible bonkers; junkies; craftspeople; Bancroft Street that my daughters called Bankrupt Street; Pennysaver Supermarket with the Chinese butchers; dogs running free, singly or in groups, waiting for masters or going to visit friends among the dog people, shitting freely everywhere; goodbye. Goodbye Berkeley Poets Co-op where my tentative poet-self had been allowed to blossom a little. The fun was over.

But I was wrong. Friends I made in those brief few months have remained my friends for life. Also, astonishingly, when the Co-op decided it was ready to publish chapbooks, they chose to do my *Once More Out of Darkness, and Other Poems* as the first of the series. I couldn't believe it. I felt incredibly honored and blessed. (I wouldn't have used the word "blessed," then, but that's what it really was.) They made it possible for a long poem of mine about pregnancy and birth to find readers. And when Rod Tulloss and I reminisced and realized how deprived both of us felt without the support of the Berkeley Poets Cooperative, the U.S. 1 Poets Co-op was born. Right here in Princeton, New Jersey, home of literary elitism, we began having meetings every Tuesday that were open to anyone who learned about us by word of mouth and walked in. Berkeley, and the spirit of inclusiveness, gave us a model. The start was rocky, there were some clashes of ego, there were some weird people walking into our meetings, but we did our best to make room for everyone. And if people walked in who didn't want to be critiqued, only praised, well, we critiqued them anyway. Gently, of course. Some of them didn't come back, some did.

U.S. 1 Poets Cooperative, begun in 1973, still exists. It still meets at somebody's home every Tuesday. It still welcomes anyone who wants to come and participate in the critique process. It has a journal and a monthly reading series at the Princeton Public Library. For years it was my lifeline. What a wonderful thing—once a week I could spend an evening with people who cared about the same thing I did—poetry. Once a week I wasn't crazy. I'd read a poem, people would comment, and whether or not I agreed with what anyone said, I'd go home energized, and the next day I'd be madly revising. By now, how many people have experienced that magic? Many dozens, for sure. Maybe more. The readings are a well-attended staple of Princeton cultural life. *U.S.1 Worksheets* now publishes an eclectic mix of poets, not only from the workshop, but from all over the USA and Canada. So Berkeley poets should check out the website and send some poems. Let what goes around come around. And the Berkeley Poets Cooperative should pat itself on the back for this long, long outreach in space and time.

JOHN GARDNER: A REMEMBRANCE

Naomi Ruth Lowinsky

If you frequented Berkeley Poets Cooperative meetings in the early 1970s, you'll remember John Gardner. He's hard to forget. He was red-haired, freckled, scrawny, with intense blue eyes—all elbows and knees, unsteady on his feet—Type I diabetes—with a blazingly brilliant mind. I can't remember whether I met John at a BPC meeting, or if it was he who introduced me to the group.

At the time, I was a lost soul wandering between the realms of the marriage I'd just left—with three young children in tow—and the poet I was trying to become. John was the first serious poet who took my poetry seriously. He was a friend, sometime lover, mentor and inspiration, initiating me into the contemplation of line length, enjambment, image, rhythm.

Do you remember his poems, how they danced and shimmied across the page without punctuation, how he punned and played with sound, how his images jumped out and bit you? He was a master. I was a grateful novice. Do you remember him sitting on the floor, reading his poems with all that intensity? Sometimes I remember us in the Berkeley brown shingle on Stuart Street where I lived. Sometimes I remember us at Charles and Maggie's place. The BPC was a nest for us both. It gave me the structure I sorely needed—the push to write a poem or two before the next meeting. It gave John an appreciative and sophisticated audience for wickedly wise poems like this one, originally published in *Small Pond #26* (1972):

HOW WE WENT TO SUNDAY SCHOOL

Dressed up
and absolutely still as glum dull windowed dressings of the
                                        absolutely silent dime-store tomb
    like corpses dressed up for the ceremonetery
    cold quarters clutched for this our offering
    hard coin to put on passed on plate of eyes to costs of having been
    dressed up
    and left there lying on the plate awaiting Service
    like cold turkey

John died many years ago. I went on to marry again, to
become a Jungian analyst, to write and publish many poems
and books. John's spirit has stayed with me. From time to time,
I dream of him. When I was working on my book *The Sister
from Below: When the Muse Gets Her Way,* which tells the story of
how poetry reclaimed me after years of focusing on profession
and family, John showed up in a powerful dream and insisted
his way into my book. In "The Sister" the muse shape shifts—
takes many forms—Eurydice, Sappho, a grandmother who died
in a concentration camp, the Ancient Naomi—all female. John
appeared and insisted that the muse could also be male, for after
all, hadn't he been my muse?

My dream is full of the color red in many shades: magenta,
burgundy, maroon, wine. I am given a poem of John's strung in
garnets, as a necklace to wear. A remembrance I have written of him
has been published in a magazine called *The Fall.* I am to conduct a
memorial service for John and to read my piece. I am dressed in red.
The ghost of John with his red hair and freckles seems to glimmer
in the air. Standing at the podium I leaf through *The Fall,* unable to
find my place. I am getting anxious.

You'll have gathered, by now, that this remembrance is my way
of making something out of that dream. There is a Jungian belief that
creating art from a dream enlivens the soul. I have found this to be
true. I've made many poems out of dreams, a number of them collected
in my book *crimes of the dreamer.*

But why, in this dream, is the magazine called *The Fall*? Perhaps it's because I've been lucky enough to live into the fall of my life, while John died in the late spring of his. Or perhaps "The Fall" has the religious meaning of a fall from grace or innocence. I've certainly lost my innocence since those early days with John and the BPC when most of us were poor and poetry was a magic carpet into fabulous realms. I had to get real about earning a living and about the hallucinatory dangers of the muse. I even gave up poetry for a few years, deciding it was "bad for my mental health."

But poetry came back and so did the spirit of John—both, I've learned, are essential to me. Maybe the dream means John is calling me from the world beyond to remember what parts of him fell into me, what parts of me fell into him. I've looked through some of the poems he wrote for me in his beautiful spidery handwriting and found two in which falling is a central image:

> I waken on fir boughs in the forest
> underneath a bawning evergreen
> sure enough there is a pixie lying by me
> she rises silent of the snow with the history of the forest
> in her eyes
> she falls into me

—*From* The Sister from Below: When the Muse Gets Her Way

John liked to make up words, thus "bawning evergreen." He had a way of using common language to evoke uncommon experience. I love "sure enough there is a pixie lying by me." And by the time we understand that she has "the history of the forest in her eyes," there is a transformation. She who falls into him is a form of the goddess.

And indeed John opened my mind and heart to the goddess as she was beginning to stir in the culture. If you are my age, you'll remember what a hard time the early 1970s were between men and women. I took my children to a daycare center run by separatist women who "did not relate to women who related to men." John was an exception. He was so frail and androgynous that nobody objected to his hanging out with the women and children. He understood all about what the patriarchy had done to women and the goddess, and supported my wildest invocations of Her being. That's an aspect of John that lives in me to this day.

Another part of John that fell into me is his ecstatic spirituality. He had such an original take on it. He'd tell me that the love songs of the '60s and '70s, the Supremes, Aretha Franklin, were about divine love brought down into the flesh. He heard it as devotional music, as mystical longing for the Beloved—a passion that lives in me still. For years I've been teaching a class at the San Francisco Jung Institute called "Deep River: Writing as Spiritual Practice," which draws inspiration from the poetry of various mystical traditions. Here's a John Gardner poem that speaks to this aspect of me:

> I dreamed I flourished back in drenching turmoils from the land
> into the ocean of you and my spirit drifted into skies of you
> to fall upon your forests and do time growing in you and begone
> returning to you I awoke for it was raining floriously out and
> freshening in upon me

> — *From* The Sister from Below: When the Muse Gets Her Way

This is not only a mystical poem, but a pagan evocation of the sacred in the natural world. I can also read it as his ongoing presence on the land, in the ocean, and the skies of me, for which I am deeply grateful.

John continues to be an inner friend and spiritual companion in "The Fall" of my life. His presence helps with the difficult task of this age: facing mortality. He certainly faced his, always knew he'd die young.

I found two untitled poems on that subject, in *Small Pond #27* (1973). They take my breath away. The first imagines decay:

> the wood of the house has shed its skin and
> being dead cries to the sun to stricken it to dust again and
> to the rain to rot it back to earth again and so they do
> the gods move in

The second is more personal, more painful, but also it seems to me, accepting. He was so young when he died—some thirty-five years ago. But perhaps for him it had already been, too long, too long.

> the last object to fall out of the ransacked night
> I was it dawned on me
> greytombed forever I did not take flight into
> I trudged off into
> dragging my empty night along behind me
> to crawl into when it had been day too long
> too long

1975

Issue #9 Contributors: Rod Tulloss, Edna Perkins, Celestine Frost, Bruce Hawkins, Alicia Ostriker, Charles Entrekin, M. Saucier, Gerald Parks, Marina LaPalma, Judith Stone, John Allen Cann, Rella Lossy, Richard Strong, Kit Duane, Ted Fleischman, Nina Rogozen, Lucille Day, Bernard Gershenson, Aaron Poller, Belden Johnson, Irene Schell, Mathilda Sorensen, Georgia Harvey, Roswell Spafford, John Hall, Michael Helm, Laura Schiff, Karen Brodine, Rena Rosenwasser, Bruce Boston.

Cover: Anthony Dubovsky
Artwork: Maggie Entrekin, Judith Stone, Betsy Gladstone Huebner, Diana Foldvary
Photo of Harriet Pierce

HIATUS IN MONTANA

Charles Entrekin

For me, personally, in 1973, I had to make a life change. I was burnt out from the long hours and the murderous commute between Berkeley and NASA in Mountain View, where I worked as the lead programmer on a huge computer project. Something had to give, and that something was me. So, I applied for and got a Teaching Assistantship in the M.F.A. program at the University of Montana, in Missoula, to study poetry under one of my favorite poets, Richard Hugo.

Co-op member, Patricia Dienstfrey, agreed to host the BPC poetry workshops at her house on Kelsey Street until I got back. So, in late August, with my wife, Maggie and my sons, Demian (9) and Caleb (3), we left Berkeley and Oregon Street and drove into the mountains. Having already completed the equivalent of a Master's degree in philosophy at the University of Alabama, and with limited funds, I was committed to completing my M.F.A. in one year.

With charismatic Richard Hugo, delicate Sister Madeline DeFrees, ex-Merry Prankster Ed McClanahan, and the whole M.F.A. program in beautiful Missoula, Montana, that year became one of the foundational supports in my appreciation and understanding of poetry and the written word. I needed that year. It changed me. We rented a house walking distance from campus, two blocks from the Clark Fork River, which froze over in winter.

My study and writing space was a basement room next to the furnace. It was a cemented-in crawl space with just enough room for a desk, light bulb, and my books. After dinner with Maggie and the boys, I would go down to my crawl space and work on my studies and my poetry. The nights got pretty cold, and all the pipes were wrapped to avoid freezing. But my study, sandwiched between those hot water pipes, was warm and completely isolated, which is what I needed for writing. I managed to get all of my academic work done and still have time left to work on my stories and poems. I found my voice, and my M.F.A. thesis became the basis for my first book, *All Pieces of a Legacy* (BPW&P, 1976).

MISSOULA SPRING

       I have become
one of my own poems.
This morning
the covered streets
opened black
in melting snow.
           I was wrong.
Winter gone, a flower
opens in me, a song, words
crawl in my veins,
a carnation of the brain,
a dogwood.

BPC Years: 1972–1974

A THERE THERE FOR POETS: BERKELEY POETS CO-OP, THE NINETEEN SEVENTIES

Patricia Dienstfrey

In an e-mail to Co-op members soliciting memories for an anthology, Charles listed some of the events in Berkeley that shaped the spirit of the Co-op's early years: the Free Speech Movement and anti-War protests, to name a few. Although, as a graduate student in City Planning, I took part in these social movements and know they influenced my adult life in important ways, it was more personal issues that led me to begin writing poetry, to seek out the Co-op and become involved. During my college years, I went through what was referred to in the sixties as "an existential breakdown," which, for me, grew out of my reading of Camus, Sartre, Dostoyevsky, and Kierkegaard. The results were a loss of feelings of connection to myself, others, things, nature, a unified world of meaning I had taken for granted in childhood. Disconnection continued to frame my experience in the early seventies, by which time I was married, the mother of three sons under five. I remained active in social issues as a volunteer at the Berkeley Free Clinic and member of a Quaker Meeting, but I was operating mostly by improvisation, habits of upbringing, and memories of childhood play and wholeness.

By the seventies, I had turned to writing as a project of self/ meaning reconstruction. At some point, a neighbor in North Oakland, where I lived with my family a few blocks from the house where Gertrude Stein grew up and of which she famously said, "There is no there there," told me about a drop-in poetry workshop. As she described it, it was in someone's house and anyone could just come in, read their poems and get helpful, supportive feedback. Amazing! Finally, I got up my nerve to go, left the children with my husband, Ted, and made it over to Charles and Maggie's, on what street in Berkeley I can't remember. It was across from a grammar school, which became my night-out-with-poetry landmark for several years. I attended a few times before I got up the courage to open my mouth.

What I knew about poetry was not much. I had dabbled in prose since college and had struggled with the way my writing came out in fragments, without reference to plot or character development. With children in my life, the fragmentation had become more profound. The poem as a short form with line breaks emerged as my only hope of making anything of the bits and pieces.

The Co-op was great! So many people who came regularly were talented and knowledgeable, and the atmosphere was attentive, nonjudgmental, and collective in the best progressive spirit of the time. So began an engagement with poetry that has been close to the center of my adulthood. As a Co-op member, I worked on the magazine and had a chance to learn about editing and layout. I picked up some publishing experience when I produced one of the Co-op's first books, Alicia Ostriker's wonderful *Once More Out Of Darkness*. For awhile, when Charles taught in Montana for a year, the Co-op met at my house. It was hectic getting the living room ready, clearing the floor of a day's layer of toys and the sofa of unfolded diapers, juggling the family dinner and bedtime schedules. Our family dog was a collie, and someone attending one night commented: "What a bourgeois dog!" I took it as a comment on the scene in general. It evoked an image of my own view of my life as divided between a commitment to exploring the disorders of writing and maintaining the orders of a household, a painful split in my life for many years, as I knew, in some fundamental way, both were worthy of my undivided attention.

By this time, I couldn't imagine life without poets and poetry, and my husband Ted at home and BPC in the community were my sources of support. But the times they were a-changing. The effects of the second wave of the Women's Movement began touching every aspect of my life as a daughter, sister, wife, mother, woman, female. And it shed new light on my reading and writing and continuing struggles with wholeness and meaning. In 1973, six women Co-op members began to meet separately—Karen Brodine, Rena Rosenwasser, Kit Duane, Laura Moriarty, Marina LaPalma, and myself. I remember that the poetry of some of these women was particularly admired in the Co-op, their talents abundantly acknowledged. Nevertheless, the six of us agreed that we experienced a division along gender lines in workshops on questions of poetics: what made a poem strong in form and content. Stating the differences in the most general terms, formally fragmented or idiosyncratic forms was not readily accepted by the men in the group; and domestic and personal content were not considered particularly interesting. The six of us wanted a chance to explore, as fully as possible, the ways our writing wanted to go and to encourage each other in freeing ourselves of negative expectations, others' and our own.

In 1970, a book entitled *The San Francisco Poets* came out, and not one woman appeared except as a companion and inspiration. The book came to stand for the absence of published women poets in the culture as a whole. As a step towards filling the void, the six of us formed Kelsey Street Press to publish the work of women who were being turned down by male-dominated small and establishment presses.

For me, the Co-op never fell into the macho camp—at least not for long. But the group, open and fluid as it was in the seventies, could not be the vehicle for what I wanted to do with writing. Co-founding Kelsey Street Press offered me a chance to work collectively to make changes in the gender profile of the published poet, the poetry reviewer, the cultural critic, the poetry teacher, and the larger writing community and world. In the writing community of communities, the Co-op continued for some years as a publisher of diverse, vital talent, of poetry that was a source of pleasure and reflection. It maintained an editorial interest in current social and political issues, such as the care of the environment. Finally, in spirit, the Co-op was generous to poets who were strangers when they walked through the door, one more cause for celebration of its thirty-one-year history.

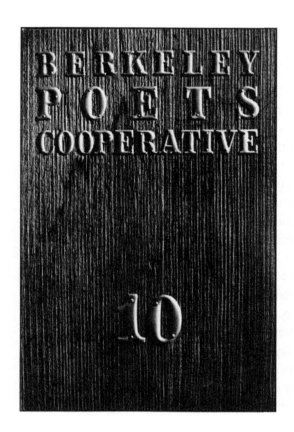

1976

Contributors: Dorothy Bryant, Peter Najarian, Michael Helm, Patricia Dienstfrey, James Margorian, Alicia Ostriker, Sheila Clare Harmon, Bruce Horovitz, Richard Marcus, Ross Figgins, Anthony Manousos, Quinton Duval, Betty Coon, Susan Swigert, Liz Socolow, Belden Johnson, Sarah Kennedy, E.W. Loomis, Loree Anderson, Marilyn King, Madeline T. Bass, Marina LaPalma, John Ceely, Bruce Boston, Marcia Falk, Joyce Greenberg, Charles Entrekin, Dorothy Swatt, Carla Christmann, Rod Tulloss, Ann Woolfolk, Betsy Gladstone Huebner, M.L. Hester, Jr., Lucille Day, Gail Gladstone, Kristin Wetterhahn

Cover: Anthony Dubovsky
Artwork: Maggie Entrekin, Betsy Gladstone Huebner, Mary Ann Hayden

Charles Klein

I have very fond memories of coming to the Berkeley Poets Cooperative at Charles and Maggie Entrekin's house across from La Conte Elementary School, circa 1970. Here was a serious group of people from all over the country who, for whatever reason, found themselves in Berkeley wanting to share and listen to others read their poetry.

I was in my early twenties and had been writing poems and songs before coming to Berkeley; being among others with like mind and spirit was confirming and comforting.

Like many people, I needed the reassurance and community offered by the Berkeley Poets Co-op. Perhaps it was a few meetings before I read. One older man said, "You sure are a poet," after I read; that was all I needed to feel accepted. I stayed with the Cooperative through four or five issues and I have written poems and songs off and on throughout my life.

I took up photography in my mid-thirties and have exhibited ever since. My photographs at their core are visual poems. They have been published worldwide. Over eighty book jackets have been designed by art directors using my images on the covers for authors, including E.L. Doctorow, Paul Auster, Richard North Patterson, Charles Baxter, Ivan Klima, Andrew Solomon, among many others.

The core assurance I got from being in the Poets Cooperative was central to my being able to raise my six children. My two birth children, Mollee and Emile, are both artists. Emile's project, *youreus*, is a U.S. identity project associated with NPR's *Snap Judgment*. He travels by bike throughout the States interviewing and painting portraits of America's diverse population.

During the past nine months, I have returned to song and poetry writing. I am currently providing lyrics for a number of musicians ranging from jazz to rap. To be able to do this in my mid-sixties comes from the practice and skill developed as a young man and through the assurance provided in consort with other poets in the BPC. To write poetry is to be able to fly. . . a lifting gift for oh-so-human a body.

BPC Years: 1972–1982

OH, THOSE '70s!

Belden Johnson

It was the Watergate autumn of 1972. I had just returned to this country after four years of dodging the draft by means of the rather ironic expedient of teaching writing for the University of Maryland on U.S. military bases throughout the world, including a stint in Long Binh, Vietnam. One of my soldier students wrote a brilliant two-liner I still remember:

> Fire extinguisher, so clean and straight,
> You must be looking for a mate.

Though I loved teaching and traveling the world, I found the Vietnam War and the Nixon years excruciating. Now I could see the famous light at the end of the tunnel. For the first time in over a decade I was *free* from the threat of having to fight in a "police action" that I judged to be illegal and morally wrong. It was as if I'd finally been able to drop a refrigerator I'd been hauling on my back.

Upon my return to these troubled shores, I purchased an old VW camper, painted blue with white clouds and festooned with madras curtains in the windows, in which to drive languorously around the country of my birth with my then-wife, Mei-yu Lo. I had no plans, other than to write. A friend had offered his home on Lake Champlain rent-free for a year, but, when we drove into Plattsburg in early October, the temperature was already down to 20° F. We headed south and were rousted by red-necked cops in Texas and then spent a lovely week with my siblings in their communal adobe on a high plateau outside Santa Fe. We got snagged in Berkeley, where I had some friends and where Mei-yu felt much more comfortable, with both the climate and the considerable Asian population.

As I walked down Telegraph Ave one cool and sunny day, I was accosted by a Walt Whitman look-alike clutching a fan of books in one claw-like hand. He had the arresting eye of The Ancient Mariner and I figured I'd better stop and placate him lest he rip my throat out with his teeth. He said his name was Bruce Hawkins and, after we'd bantered a bit, he invited me to the meeting of the Poets Cooperative that evening.

I showed up at Charles and Maggie Entrekin's house on Oregon Street and met another Bruce, this one a Boston, and a lovely woman who called herself Marina LaPalma, as well as a few others whose names I apologize for forgetting. People read their poems aloud and received what was usually constructive criticism. Not having brought a poem, I was inspired to jot one down on the spot. I called it "Evening Prayer":

> we nursed the old pontiac
>   along the Golden Horn
> until something clanked below
>   & we ground down beside a seawall.
> wolfgang slid under the chassis
>   like a fat slug of grease
> & began screaming for tools.
>   keough took the black briefcase
> containing his three unpublished novels
>   & stepped over the wall mumbling in gaelic.
> the water closed like hissing elevator doors
>   over his head. By the time I
> looked up the sun had dipped below Istanbul
>   & the whole city was golden. I wept.
> my tears crawled up the minarets
>   into the muezzins' throats
> until they staggered, drunk, out along
>   the filaments of their song.

Anything could happen at those meetings. One evening, a poet calling himself Peter Pussydog stood with great solemnity to read a poem he called "Candy":

> I never saw the movie
> but I ate the book.

He sat down to, first, a stunned silence and then laughter and applause.

Over my ten years in the Cooperative, I wrote a number of poems during the meetings, which I found at least as inspiring as those I'd experienced at the University of Iowa Writers' Workshop, where I'd earned an M.F.A. in fiction. The Co-op gave me a chance to explore a different genre. Eventually I had accumulated enough passable poems to be published in a chapbook whose title, *Snake Blossoms*, I owe to Bruce Boston. A Co-op friend who worked at Cody's Bookstore at the time, Dorothy Swatt (aka Dorothy Wall), told me it sold out faster than any book of poetry had ever done there, no doubt due to its racy cover.

I took a couple of turns as one of the editors for the magazine and even hawked them on the street. I loved reading Mary Oliver's submissions of her early stories to the magazine, which we judged less exciting than her poems. I became good friends with Susan Stern and Roz Spafford and Mike Helm. Mike published my early essays on relationships in *City Miner*. These evolved into my recent book, *Real Relationship: Essential Tools to Help You Go the Distance*, available on Amazon. I was honored to know the marvelous poet Karen Brodine before cancer stole her from us. I benefited from the live feedback to my work I got at the meetings, and I learned whose critiques to trust. I enjoyed participating in live readings with Charles and other poets in San Francisco. I got to be in a photo for the *NY Times* article on us, when I had hair to my shoulders and wore a hand-crafted Elizabethan shirt.

I look back fondly on those years in Berkeley, when I went through some momentous changes, including an amiable divorce, primal therapy, and then training to become a therapist. I worked in a daycare center while doing that training and had two children of my own. I also wrote a couple of novels, one of which, *Fathers and Teachers*, received insightful feedback from both Charles and Bruce B. Through it all, the Co-op was an ever-fixed mark, a pole star of my life, a place where I felt at home. Thank you, fellow members.

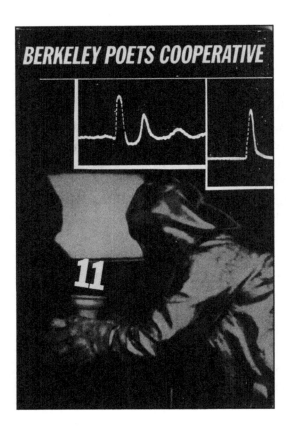

1977

Contributors: Dorothy Swatt, Susan Fromberg Schaeffer, Sue Swigert, Bruce Boston, Stan Rice, Mar Lane, Ted Fleischman, Mona Simpson, Betty Coon, David Lampert, Violet Gregory, Debra Barnhart, Stewart Florsheim, Jan Glading, Alicia Ostriker, Belden Johnson, Stephanie Saloman, Carla Christmann, Joyce Odam, Anne S. Perlman, Rod Tulloss, Michael Covino, Betsy Gladstone Huebner, Chris Bahr, Lucy Day, Rona Spalten, Charles Entrekin, Peter Najarian, Anthony Dubvosky.

Cover and artwork: Anthony Dubovsky

REMEMBERING THE BERKELEY POETS CO-OP

Marcia Falk

> Two plums, three . . .
> butter on a seashell, a chunk of cheese . . .
> [something something something] a yard of weeds . . .

> —*Remembered fragments of a poem written in Betsy's kitchen*

I have one of the worst memories I've heard of in a middle-aged woman. Much worse than that of, say, my friend Lucy Day, who remembers, in stunning detail, not only her own past but the pasts of many acquaintances with whom she has had friendly—or in some cases not-so-friendly—encounters. Without the bits of information fed to me by Lucy, whom I met at the first meeting I attended of the Berkeley Poets Co-op and with whom I have remained close for coming-up-on four decades, I would not have been able to put together the pieces of this remembrance.

Even when something is very important to me, as the Co-op was, and is, I have little recall of factual details—or, I should say, details that approximate facts, since, as we know, factuality doesn't exist, least of all in the memory, which is always playing catch with the imagination. But impressions do stay with me, mostly in the form of sensations, like colors—the green of Betsy Huebner's breakfast table, for example. (Or was it only the view of her back yard from her kitchen window that was green?) Like the sensation of Betsy herself—her good-hearted daffiness, her jubilance, her funny hats. (Or did she only begin wearing hats in later years, when she became an Orthodox Jew?) Betsy, who was loathe to criticize poems even when they urgently needed it, who was quick to respond with effusive praise to the poems that other poets had critiqued. Betsy could drive me crazy with her total lack of criticalness. But now that she's gone—she died in 2011—I see her contributions to the workshops in a new way: I appreciate her support of, and respect for, the creativity of others. I wish I'd spent more time in her presence.

Charles Entrekin, too, wore hats; I can still picture him in a modified cowboy hat. (I think I remember that, but I may have invented it.) Big man, broad smile, slight Southern drawl. My first night at the Co-op—Lucy tells me it was at Charles's house—Charles was so gracious, in a Southern sort of way, that I almost stopped shaking in my Frye boots. I'll always remember the sensation of being welcomed and invited to read my poems to a roomful of strangers, all of them poets. Poets! I introduced myself and read, voice quaking. Lucy says that the crowd—and it sure did feel to me like a crowd; had there been only two people in the room it would still have felt like a crowd, that's how nervous I was—liked my poems. I don't recall a word that was said, just that I went home relieved and determined not to give up on writing. Before that night, I hadn't been sure I was a poet; no, I was sure I was an impostor. The Co-op members made me feel— and continued over the coming meetings to make me feel—like the real thing.

Some people made particularly strong impressions—Pat Dienstfrey, for instance, whose brilliant way of "telling it slant" continues to fascinate me today. And still others, whose diverse sensibilities were revealed in their poems, much as in their personalities. But my strongest impression was—is—of the group as a whole, which gave me a home.

I was in the Co-op only a few months. (Or maybe it was only weeks; my sense of chronology is no better than the rest of my memory.) I don't remember how I found out about the Co-op, just that it was in the summer of 1973, shortly after I had moved to Berkeley from Palo Alto to collaborate with the Yiddish poet Malka Heifetz Tussman on a translation of her poems. At summer's end I was off to Jerusalem, for what was to be a year spent finishing my translation of the Song of Songs, the basis of my doctoral dissertation.

As it turned out, life had other plans. A war broke out ten days after I arrived in Israel, and I was not to do any dissertation writing that year. This would be another story entirely, except for the fact that the Co-op continued to be an important presence in my life during this traumatic time. Amidst the shock and disorientation of living in a country at war—streets bare of men between the ages of seventeen and fifty, bus routes canceled, universities and libraries closed, windows of all the houses shuttered at night to keep the city invisible to enemy planes—amidst this upheaval, which was coupled with the loneliness of someone new to her surroundings, a letter arrived one day bearing impossibly unexpected news. The Co-op magazine, which had published my work in several issues, had been contacted by the editors of two anthologies for permission to reprint my poems. Would I agree? The request came from Lucy and was accompanied by a thrilling congratulation. I felt embraced: the Co-op was happy for me. Among all the intense sensations of that war-scarred year, I remember with fondness the glow I felt upon opening that letter.

When I returned to the States, I began my first full-time academic job, at the State University of New York at Binghamton, and the dissertation was put off for another two years. The weather in Binghamton was so gloomy, and I was so terrified of failure in my new grown-up role and so lonesome for my Jerusalem and California friends, including those I had met through the Co-op, that, as often as I could, I flew back like a homing pigeon to Berkeley. I lived in communal houses on Regent Street and Hillegass, hung out at the Med smoking cigarettes and sipping mugs of hot milk with orgeat, and met up with friends at the Bateau Ivre for late-night glasses of wine, where we talked philosophy, politics, and, of course, poetry. The Co-op continued to welcome me and to publish my poems in the magazine. I felt a part of things.

Eventually, upon threat of being fired from my job, I managed to get the thesis finished. It was time to leave Berkeley for good and return to the real world. I remember the pit in my stomach when this realization sunk in. I was devastated to have to leave.

And astonishingly—or maybe it's not all that astonishing—having bounced back and forth between two continents and the two coasts of this one for several decades, I now find myself nestled back in Berkeley, just a few blocks from where my first encounter with the Co-op took place. If I were to lean out the west-facing window of the top floor of my house right now, I might even be able to see Charles and Maggie Entrekin's former house on Oregon Street, where I felt like a poet for the first time.

BERKELEY POETS COOPERATIVE/12

1977

Contributors: Richard Strong, Lyn Lifshin, Susan Hoffman, Lorna Bennett, Kathleen Lignell, Frank Polite, Jeff Harris, Nick Johnson, Jack Finefrock, Alicia Ostriker, Linda McCloud, JoAnn Ugolini, Mario Donatelli, Cliff Fyman, Bruce Hawkins, Dorothy Swatt, Betty Coon, Carla Christmann, Charles Entrekin, Alice Fulton, Ted Fleischman, Belden Johnson, Stephen Ford Brown, Michael Covino, Elizabeth Brown, Stewart Florsheim, Dennis Holzman, Susan Swigert Strong, Thaisa Frank, Michael Covino, John Krich, Bruce Boston

Cover: Anthony Dubovsky
Artwork: Maggie Entrekin

HUNGER

Marilyn King

Ah yes, I remember it well. Driving to Berkeley from my home in southern Alameda County for hits of culture I needed more than I knew.

I was in love with a Catholic monk at the time, who was also a poet. It was back in the early seventies when he wrote flaming love poems to me, which inspired my earliest attempts to commit passion to paper. Since he was a celibate, there was a lot to write. So we continued doing so, as a result of not doing it, for a long time. Then he was ordained, and we headed for the East Bay Regional parks to do it.

Before that time, I'd started attending meetings of the BPC, though in no way could I rightly call myself a poet, but I tried. I would commute up to Charles's house with my latest impassioned drivel in hand. My priest loved what I wrote; why didn't BPC? I often drove home in tears, so outclassed was I by BPC members.

I hadn't been an English undergrad major, as it seemed they all had, alluding to the works of famous poets during meetings. I'd been a sociology undergrad major and was hustling to support two kids as a social worker with Head Start. I wrote a lot there about taking kids to doctors and dentists, compiling immunization charts, preparing their health records for kindergarten.

After more than two years together, the priest and I finally became engaged. For one-and-a-half days we anticipated marriage and broke up in a fit of terror.

I continued driving to Berkeley, determined to become a poet. I remember Belden, Bruce Boston, Karen Brodine, Charles Entrekin, Marina LaPalma, Alicia Ostriker, and a few faces without names. I remember a line from a poem written by one handsome fellow who described another as a "wired-up marshmallow," a term I've resisted plagiarizing for 30-plus years, for which I think I deserve some credit. They were good, those Berkeley poets. I surely represented an embarrassment to them, so I was surprised when they included in Issue #10 my first published poem, "Hunger."

In 1976, my kids and I moved to Marin to live with my next lover, who turned out, after eighteen months of cohabitation, to be gay. . . or bi-. . . or something else I didn't understand. I think he wanted a family, so he put up with me in order to play Papa to my kids. That gave me a lot to write about.

In 1983, I entered grad school at SF State pursuing an M.A. in creative writing. Working full time tutoring English students at a community college learning center, I tended my own coursework at night, which meant an exhausting schedule. I was working on a novel/thesis when I came down with chronic mononucleosis, which meant leaving both classes at SF State and my tutoring job, and finally resorting to permanent Social Security disability for an income. Fortunately, by then my kids were grown and gone.

After having written no poetry for twenty-five years, I saw a poster in a local coffeehouse window advertising monthly meetings of Poetry Farm. So I wrote a poem about what I thought of the Iraq war, which I read timidly at my first meeting with the group. They loved it, and the MC yelled, "We have a new farmer!" And I was off and writing. From there I joined the Marin Poetry Center, which boasts about 300 members, including two former U.S. Poet Laureates: Robert Haas and Kay Ryan. MPC began publishing me regularly in their annuals, as did Poetry Farm. Poetry, it would seem, was more in keeping with the energy level of a chronic *mono* patient than was a novel.

A while ago, after reading an announcement in the Marin Poetry Center newsletter, I saw the name Charles Entrekin listed as a scheduled reader at 333 Caledonia in Sausalito, a venue I knew well. So I attended, reconnected with Charles, and read some poems from the Berkeley Poets Co-op Issue #10, two by Charles and one by me, the first poem I ever had published.

Now I'm working on my first chapbook, and to this day, I e-mail my poems for friendly critique to a friend, an ex-priest turned Ph.D., now married for the fifth time.

Below is "Hunger," which appeared in Issue #10 of the Berkeley Poets Cooperative, and which gave me the courage not to give up on writing poetry.

HUNGER

Woke up ready this morning.
Wasn't too sure about my head,
but my body was erased and corrected
and really quite adequate.

I locked the back door three times,
watered the dried flower arrangement,
threw the bag of cat food in the washer,
and went out at 4:00 P.M. to greet the morning.

Walking, I noticed
everybody looked like a pair of arms.
I could see through the walls of houses
that they were filled with hearths
and down quilts handmade by grandmothers
who over-fed everybody from kitchens
smelling of cinnamon.
Each green field I passed
was an envelope for me to lie in
and figure out
where to mail myself.

Overwhelmed by hunger,
I ate myself sick on dinner out
and went home to bed, strangely tired,
where I watched TV
in the mirror
with the sound off.

BERKELEY POETS COOPERATIVE/14

1978

Contributors: Ted Fleischman, Charles Entrekin, Carla Kandinsky, Susan Strong, Rod Tulloss, Belden Johnson, Burghild Holzer, Jazan Higgins, Bruce Hawkins, Betsy Huebner, Michael Covino, Mary Lane, Lucille Day, Bruce Boston, Gus Gustafson, Stewart Florsheim, Dorothy Swatt, JoAnn Ugolini, David Lampert, Sharon Williams, Betty Coon, Sarah Kirsch, Maggie Entrekin, Anna West, Peter Najarian, Charles Entrekin, Michael Covino

Cover: Anthony Dubovsky
Artwork: Jo Ann Ugolini

2325 BLAKE AND 1733 VIRGINIA STREET

Charles Entrekin

After returning from Montana, we rented a sea captain's house on Blake Street that became BPC's home for about a year. Then, with two new jobs in hand—teaching Creative Writing at Contra Costa Junior College (nights), and a financially successful computer consulting gig in San Francisco (days)—Maggie and I bought a house in North Berkeley, 1733 Virginia Street, which became the new home address for the workshops of the Berkeley Poets Cooperative.

Suddenly, we owned one of those painted ladies, an old Victorian, a shaky, stately old home with lots of charm and few modern conveniences. First thing we did was repaint it in colors from the palette of Maggie Entrekin, earth tones of mauve and purple and rust-red. And our "painted lady" was located in an area, as one older resident claimed, that was once known as the "golden triangle of Berkeley," an area bounded by Shattuck, University, Gilman, and the Bay, where, supposedly, creativity flourished most readily. I liked that and I chose to believe it.

So the Co-op, now stable with a new address, began to expand its horizons and we began to publish chapbooks as well as magazines, starting with *Once More Out of Darkness and other poems* by Alicia Ostriker (1974, and reprinted 1976), soon followed by Karen Brodine's wonderful book, *Slow Juggling*, and then Bruce Hawkins' amazing *Wordrows* and my own *All Pieces of a Legacy*.

In 1975, the BPC formed a working relationship with Don Cushman and the West Coast Print Center, and with our new cover designer, artist Anthony (Tony) Dubovsky. Don Cushman cared about the art and the craft of the printer, and with help from the West Coast Print Center, our magazines and chapbooks began to take on the look and feel of an established, well-crafted product. Tony managed or designed most of our covers (magazines and chapbooks), from Issue #9 through Issue #30, from 1975 through 1989, a span of 14 years. Tony was a strong member of the Co-op, and his work provided us, issue by issue, with an artistically coherent presentation of design excellence.

In the spring of 1976, we got a call from a freelance journalist, Kenneth Lamott, who said he wanted to interview us for an article he wanted to write. Lamott spoke to several members of the Co-op and followed Bruce Hawkins around Berkeley with his camera taking photographs of Bruce selling the magazine on Telegraph Avenue. He also took photographs of us at the West Coast Print Center. All of us were busy at that time, and didn't think too much about it. That year, we had established the Co-op as a magazine and a press[1]. As the Co-op became successful, more people became involved. Then on August 15, 1976, Kenneth Lamott's article on the Co-op made the cover of the *New York Times Magazine*.

The following Wednesday, I came home from work and discovered my front yard filled with people trying to get in to the Berkeley Poets Co-op meeting. There was a line leading up to the front door. We had become famous and suddenly there was standing room only in our living room. New writers showed up, but also people who were just passing through town, who came out of sheer curiosity. For a time, we had to rent a neighbor's huge empty room just for Co-op meetings.

That was an exciting time. Standing room only, the whole house filled with people asking for directions to the bathroom. We had to purchase an industrial-sized coffee pot. People were coming from far and wide to be part of it. Early on, when there were only ten or twelve of us, we were pretty informal. We used to organize work parties to do layout, and we would assemble the magazines and chapbooks

---

[1] The Co-op became a Berkeley institution receiving awards from The National Endowment for the Arts, the Berkeley Arts Council and the California Arts Council, and garnering acclaim in such publications as the *Daily Cal* (04/1974), The *San Francisco Magazine* (1974), The *Berkeley Monthly* (9/30/1976, 02/1981), Berkeley *Daily Gazette* (3/9/1976), *California Living* (4/15/1979), the *New York Times Magazine* (8/29/1976), the *Berkeley Express* (6/27/80), *The New York Times Book Review* (2/18/83), and the *Village Voice* (1/19/1989).

around a huge Mexican table. Everyone pitched in. We drank wine, sang, danced, and marched around that giant brown table, collating, stacking, and then staple-binding and boxing. That was our production process for quite a while.

But then, in 1976, with growth and acclaim and financial success, we had to organize. Also, suddenly we were able to pay the extra costs for shrink wrapping and perfect binding, and we could afford quality printing.

The BPC had become an ongoing, thriving enterprise.

1978

Contributors: Marcia Falk, Charles Entrekin, Barry Alpert, Randall Nicholas, Sharon Williams, Ramsay Bell, George Mattingly, Rod Tulloss, Bruce Hawkins, Michael Covino, Jazan Higgins, Gus Gustafson, Bruce Boston, Beau Beausoleil, Jo Ann Ugolini, William Zander, Albert Huffstickler, Phyllis Koestenbaum, Adriano Spatola, Ted Fleischman, Robin Gajdusek, Betsy Huebner, Susan C. Strong, Burghild Holzer, Percy Warner Lea, Dorothy Swatt, Al Ferber, Edward Martinez, Hilda Johnson, Luis Garcia, Linda McCloud

Cover: Anthony Dubovsky
Artwork: Betsy Huebner

A TIME, A PLACE

Dorothy Wall

I remember my first time at the Berkeley Poets Co-op in 1975, which at that time met in Charles and Maggie Entrekin's living room in their house on Blake Street. The room was large and artsy, a brass double bed at one end, Maggie's easel at the other. Her figurative paintings, colorful and energetic, were stacked around the room. The walls were being painted, with large brush strokes of two different shades of blue/green, as if Maggie hadn't decided which one she liked. There were lots of potted plants, a bench, a couch, I don't remember what else. My daughter Lisa went to Graham Cracker School on Benvenue, which Belden and his wife Gail ran, and Belden had told me about the BPC workshop when I learned he was a poet and mentioned I wrote poetry, too.

So here I was in my bell bottom jeans, turtleneck and denim vest, poems in hand, nervous. Fifteen or twenty people milled around, waiting for things to start. I sat on the bench next to the overstuffed couch where a brightly dressed man and woman were seated, he in a blousy shirt, she in a long skirt. I introduced myself and learned they had just come down from the mountains and her name was Rain and his was Bow. As I sat there next to Rain and Bow, I looked around the room at a man in a cowboy hat (Mike Helm) sitting on the floor leaning against a large planter, at bearded Belden in his overalls, at Charles and Maggie chatting, at all the art and poetry in the room, and thought, "Wow, this is the place to be."

I was responding to the hippie flavor, the creativity, the "cool." (We'll overlook Rick Moody's observation that if you have to talk about cool, you are not it.) It was perfect for me, just stepping out of my marriage and excited about writing and about building a new network of friends and connections. It was an expansive time, and the BPC was both a stimulating gathering place and a doorway, part of a burgeoning Bay Area arts scene, interlinked with other small presses, independent booksellers, high-quality printers, nonprofit arts groups, grant organizations. If you wanted to get involved in the BPC—helping to edit and produce the magazine, organize readings, write grants—you were inevitably connected to this web of Bay Area writers and artists.

I soon found myself, as production editor of the magazine, traipsing over to the West Coast Print Center off Ashby Avenue, where the oily smell of ink and hulking, noisy machines captivated me. It was an inked-stained place, stacks of prints everywhere, run by Don Cushman and specializing in high quality offset and letter-press printing, part of a Bay Area movement for printing as an art form. While ordinary traffic whizzed by, inside the warren of rooms the WCPC revived the art of elegant letter-press broadsides, prints and books. Beautiful fonts, each letter imprinted in the paper's textured mesh, a dash of color–a poem wasn't just a poem but a visual pleasure. I went home that day with a poster of bird-of-paradise for my bedroom, a misprint Don handed me casually when I admired it, and a fascination for these off-the-track, hidden places that seemed to riddle the Bay Area. One afternoon I ended up singing "Happy Birthday" with a crowd of writers and filmmakers renting space in an Emeryville warehouse. Another day I met with Joyce Jenkins who put out *Poetry Flash*, the listing of Bay Area literary events, in her postage-stamp-sized home office next to Berkeley's Bateman Park. I headed whenever I could to Small Press Traffic on San Pablo Avenue, a large, unadorned room stocked with hundreds of small press books regular bookstores wouldn't sell. I was always taken aback by the sheer number of volumes, both excited—so much creativity—and unnerved—who needs another poet!

The beauty of the BPC was that it was both a press and a workshop. As a press, it was a group of committed writers putting out a magazine and poetry books. As a workshop, it was open to the public, providing a constant flow of new blood and diversity. No one else was doing this. There were private writing groups, or poetry classes—I took one with Alta, the local feminist poet famous for the picture of her naked with a Kotex pad. But this group was part of the community, eclectic, with all kinds of people filtering in and out.

Once the *New York Times* article profiling the BPC came out in August 1976, the workshop overflowed. No longer able to squeeze into Charles and Maggie's living room on Virginia Street, the workshop moved up the block to a larger rented room sectioned off from a house, with an outdoor entrance just off the street. Shag rug, pillows, a toilet in a low-ceilinged closet.

The room would be jammed on workshop nights, standing room only, people leaning against window sills. I remember a lot of jeans, beaded earrings, a woman with feathers in her braids, a university professor beating out the rhythm of a poem with a street poet. When someone read, the energy would go quiet, taut. I have an image of Betsy Huebner standing in the doorway to read in a blue dress and pith helmet, and another time brandishing a rubber glove. Not sure what that was about, but her work always made me listen. I couldn't get a fix on Ted Fleischman's whimsical work—was it even a poem? I didn't know, awash in the newness of all these voices.

Bruce Hawkins' understated lyricism—I always loved hearing his poems. He was the dedicated member who sold our magazine from his backpack on the streets of Berkeley in his quiet, unassuming way, holding out a book, that slight tilt to his bearded face. Michael Covino, blonde, boyish, the one who came to meetings in khaki pants and a button-down shirt. Cross-legged on the carpet, his whole body would lean into his intense interrogations of a poem, a poet. After I read a short prose poem, four or five sentences, his voice cut across the room to me. "It's a nice moment, but it doesn't go anywhere."

"I like it," a woman volunteered, half-lying against an over-sized floor pillow.

"Why?" This from Covino.

"I don't know. I just do."

More people leapt in. References to Nabokov, "Caress the detail, the divine detail." Arguments about said detail.

I examined my words on the page. What's wrong with a poem being a moment? Does it have to go somewhere? What's the difference between an undeveloped poem and a fragment? I had to think about that. I'm still thinking about that.

There were skirmishes, high-voltage exchanges. Certain personalities could infuse a meeting with an edge that put other people off, the risk of an open-door policy. I learned from them all, and from Charles' wry, relaxed comments in his Southern accent, as he kept the workshop rolling forward. He had one foot in the university as a creative writing instructor, and the other in the community, and this is what appealed to me. Smart, informed, but unpretentious.

By 1976, I was commuting out to the M.A. program in creative writing at San Francisco State, and in 1977 began working at Cody's Books. It wasn't an easy time—divorce, work, school, single-parenthood—but I was delightfully saturated in language, books, poems, ideas. I used to walk into Cody's when the morning sun poured through those lofty plate-glass windows and run my hands over the amazing array of books for the sheer pleasure. At S.F. State, I found excellent and stimulating teachers–Stan Rice, Kathleen Fraser–and a few stand-out students who challenged me. But it was at the BPC that the exchanges were poet-to-poet, among a group of peers, and something was let loose that didn't happen in the classroom. More hands-on, more intuitive maybe. More personal. We were in it together. And no grades.

Some thought the BPC should be something other than what it was, more urban, feminist, cutting-edge, or experimental. Some thought the group was shaped too much by Charles's university-honed aesthetic. Though we believed in an egalitarian ethos, even egalitarian groups have power structures, they're just more covert. It was clear Charles was the glue. If you weren't comfortable with the university/community hybrid, you moved on.

I don't remember when I stopped going to BPC workshops; it was sometime in the early '80s. M.A. in hand, I had set out on the part-time teaching circuit, picking up a creative writing class or two at several Bay Area colleges to patch together full-time work at a starvation wage. A slog, but I was teaching college creative writing as I had always wanted. And, commuting from San Francisco to Napa to Contra Costa, hosting sleepovers for 12-year-olds, mowing the lawn, writing poems and reviews. I was too overloaded to keep up with the BPC, and on to other things. Our lives seemed to be going that way—my friends and I settled down, partnered or re-partnered. There were fewer parties, more focus on kids and work.

I don't know that the BPC could have happened any other time. We were young, idealistic. We believed in a cooperative spirit, in art and expression as a valuable, even essential, part of the self, of a culture. We would nurture that spirit in each other and in our community. And along the way, make enduring friends, party, read poetry in bed to a new lover, sharpen our thinking and wrestle with those perennial questions about what makes a piece of writing indelible. I think that's cool.

1979

Contributors: Ramsay Bell, David Kirby, William Tychonievich, Alice Glarden Brand, Ted Fleischman, Michael Covino, Noelle Caskey, Liz Socolow, Stewart Florsheim, Betsy Huebner, Lucille Day, Charles Entrekin, Susan C. Strong, Bruce Hawkins, Joyce Odam, Dennis W. Folly, Marian Keeler, Carla Kandinsky, Ivan Argüelles, Jillane Allison Gaspar, Gus Gustafson, Mary R. Rudge, Paula Friedman, Sharon Williams, Richard Strong, Bruce Boston, Oren Eisenberg, Jan Glading, Alicia Ostriker, Samuel Gross, Betty Coon, Norman Moser, Jo Ann Ugolini, Judith Stephens

Cover: Anthony Dubovsky
Artwork Anne Hawkins

COMMUNAL LIFE IN BERKELEY

Peter Najarian

[The following is an excerpt from an unpublished memoir in creative
nonfiction. It is narrated by Pete Najarian, in regard to the autumn of
1971, when he lived in a commune in Berkeley. His fictional book about
this commune, *Wash Me On Home, Mama,* was published by the Co-op in
1978. The names in the following excerpt, except those of the Cheeseboard
founders, have been changed to protect the privacy of those involved.]

"Oh, it feels so good to come home and rest," said the beautiful
Vivian, a sister arriving home from her rehearsal with her theater
group, The East Bay Sharks.

One night, Vivian would cook a delicious leek and potato soup.
On another night, Jewel cooked minestrone. Sarah prepared an
aubergine dish. Shana concocted a Greek lemon drop soup, and the
next night Alan made a stir-fry. Donald, longing for "food that sticks to
your ribs," used his turn for chuck beef and "spuds."

"Look at everyone's faces, aren't they beautiful?" Jewel whispered in
my ear one dinnertime, everyone holding hands around the big table
with their faces glowing like angels in the candlelight.

"This is where I live," Dan and Sarah's son Saul said, and his friend
said, "It looks like Treasure Island."

An older man named Clear came by one day to lend a hand after
he learned of our "experiment." He had been a nuclear physicist before
dropping out, and he helped us install an old pay phone so the dime
came back after each call.

Another day, a mysterious neighbor contributed by leaving a bag of
vegetables by the side door. Molly's sister's boyfriend worked on a tuna
boat in Alaska, and they visited with dozens of tuna steaks.
Sahag and Elizabeth Avedisian, who had started a tiny shop called The
Cheeseboard, extended their collective into a "cheese conspiracy" so
"the people" could buy cheese at wholesale prices, and our commune
store was used to cut and distribute it.

Shana, Donald, Alan, and Sol each had an inheritance like Jewel's; Tim and Ryan had savings that could last a while; Molly, Brawley, and Teddy did carpentry jobs; Vivian performed in little theaters, like the old garage called *Freight and Salvage*; Jill clerked part-time; and young Cindy was a welfare worker.

We shared all the work. I lined the compost with tin after the rats frightened Molly, Tim built a barrier for the dogs after Ryan complained about the shit, Brawley set a potter's kiln in one of the garages for the neighbor, Miriam, who was going to teach us pottery, but later had an affair with Donald instead.

I stopped by my old home on Addison Street and, pausing by my Underwood, I touched the keys like a pianist who didn't play anymore; some part of me, deeper than my need for a woman, wanted to stay and stare out the window. Would I ever write again?

We were visited one day by a bearded and barefoot longhair from The Free Bakery, a collective that let anyone bake free one day a week, and Sarah fried eggs for him, as if he were a fellow immigrant from the same homeland. He had heard that Sarah and I had been looking for an oven, and he offered the one in his collective on Grove Street in West Oakland, because they were about to be evicted. It was from a Navy ship in Alameda and as big as an elephant and painted black and yellow in glossy enamel like a giant treasure chest. But it weighed over four tons and no one knew how to move it, until Tim said, with his love of giant projects, that we could move it with a "come-along."

"If you know the right levers," he said, with the wild look he always flashed whenever he was excited, "you can move a whole country!"

Friday night, October 29, Ryan and Sarah baked potatoes in the cool moonlight and barbecued the tuna steaks caught in Alaska, but their turn for dinner was interrupted. The man who promised us the oven, Tom Morrison, came back and said there was a shootout after the police had suddenly raided the Free Bakery for marijuana, and everyone but he was busted. Our commune, Tom Morrison said, should go and take whatever we needed from his collective or the landlord would get it. We rented a big U-Haul for the coming Sunday.

Inept with anything mechanical, I watched while the other men pried apart the four oven sections with a long pole, then I helped carry each section to the U-Haul in the misty drizzle. We actually ended up moving the whole four-ton oven with nothing but our hands, like cave people with a mammoth. I had already helped Tim mold a foundation in the store, and we bolted the oven back as easily as we had taken it apart.

Then how alive it seemed, with its big round presence, like a giant Buddha in a temple. We were actually going to have a bakery and bake bread and let others come and bake as well. I had lived since childhood in cities of steel, but this was the first time I was part of what humans could do with their hands. What a brave new world we seemed to live in!

But Molly and Dan were breaking up. She had been crying on the day the visitor came to offer the oven. Dan had a serious talk with Sarah, also, about their son Saul; and Teddy and Jill had problems with their child, too; and Cindy was jealous about Brawley's ex-wife, who had dropped by unannounced; and Sol felt alone while Jewel slept with me; and Vivian swung up and down with her musician boyfriend; and Donald had to move his wolves from the hills. I, however, felt at peace as long as I was sleeping with Jewel.

November arrived with each of us returning to our separate beds, and a different world lay between our legs, as if the oven was just another dream. It was raining hard by then, and our commune was falling apart, the bread-less oven a lonely Buddha no one would visit anymore.

Another group of people would eventually carry it to somewhere else after I left, and I would never learn what happened to it. And whatever else would disappear when the journal was left in the rain and the ink bled into oblivion, our youth and our need to build a home, not just on the corner of Bancroft and Grant Streets, but in the universe itself, persevered.

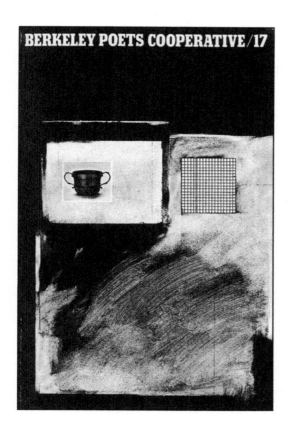

BERKELEY POETS COOPERATIVE/17

1980

Contributors: Dennis W. Folly, Hilda Johnston, Dorothy Wall, Charles Entrekin, Ramsay Bell, Carla Kandinsky, Bruce Boston, Michael Covino, John Ceely, Theresa Bacon, Stewart Florsheim, Liz Socolow, Lois Bunse, Carolyn Drewes, Nona Nimnicht, Madeine T. Bass, Sharon Williams, Randall Nicholas, Ted Fleischman, Lucille Day, Bruce Hawkins, JoAnn Ugolini, Robert Taylor, Jr.

Cover: Anthony Dubovsky
Artwork: Maggie Entrekin

FINDING COMMON GROUND

Stewart Florsheim

I arrived in Berkeley in 1976 after living in The Netherlands for
a couple of years. I moved to Amsterdam after college, and was lucky
enough to land a job at a publishing company. I came back to attend the
Master's Program in Creative Writing at San Francisco State, but I also felt
that Berkeley might be the only stateside match for Amsterdam. After all,
where else in the U.S. could students strike, people smoke pot openly,
and writers publish whatever they wanted in periodicals like *The Berkeley
Barb?* To my chagrin, I quickly realized that all these activities were
reactions to what was going on at the time in the U.S., whereas in The
Netherlands, they were just part of an old, civilized society.

To say that I was disoriented would be a gross understatement.
I returned to the states via Asia, where I took a three-month trip,
traveling overland from New Delhi to Istanbul. Part of the trip included
a trek through the Himalayas, where I saw the most breathtaking sights
I had ever seen. I went through Afghanistan, where I saw the gigantic
Buddha before it was blown up by the Taliban. I also saw abject
poverty, and experienced illness and violence. It was the kind of trip
that shook me to my core. I was anxious to settle down, but had lost
my bearings. A simple trip to the supermarket proved overwhelming,
with all the aisles and choices to be made.

I tried to settle into Berkeley life. I found a flat to share, attended
classes, and was fortunate to land a job at Cody's, the legendary
bookstore on Telegraph Avenue. I remember how impressed I was
by the poetry section. Not just a few rows of books, but an entire
section—and Cody's had one of the most well-respected poetry
reading series in the country. My brother-in-law played basketball with
Charles Entrekin, and told me I might want to check out his poetry
cooperative. *Just a bunch of crazy poets who read their work to each other.
You'll fit right in.*

I attended my first meeting with the same amount of skepticism I
had started to feel towards Berkeley. Even though I had been there for

just a few weeks, I started to experience the seedy side of Telegraph Avenue, and see the poverty in the flatlands. One of my flatmates turned out to be a pathological liar; the other one spent a bit too much time in his room alone with his cat. I thought the Co-op might be too "touchy-feely" after being in more formal workshops on the East Coast.

I was wrong. At my first meeting, I was struck, not just by the openness, but by the spirit of collaboration. Someone read, and then the discussion began. The feedback was usually incisive and constructive. We discussed imagery, language, sound. We mulled over words. I read my poem towards the end. It was a poem about traveling in India, and I thought it was done. *Close,* everyone concluded, *but it needs some more work.* I finally agreed.

I've been in many workshops over the years, and what strikes me now about the Co-op is that everyone was invested in making the poem succeed. The honesty was often brutal, but the intention was unmistakable. The word *cooperative* took on a new meaning. We often deconstructed and reconstructed enough to arrive at the poem's literal core.

Of course, part of the motive was to produce the best work possible. We published a magazine on a regular basis, and wanted it to be excellent. Each issue was edited by a different member of the Co-op, to distribute the responsibility as well as the accountability. To complete the cycle, the magazines were sold on a street corner by Bruce Hawkins, a longtime member of the Co-op. He made a modest living selling our work.

We had our own artistic ecosystem. I started to feel comfortable enough to invite other poet-friends to our meetings, like Nina Burghild Holzer and Jazan Higgins. I met my lifelong friend, David Lampert, there. All of us shared the most intimate details of our lives. We laughed and cried together. We played softball and had some great parties. Many of us paired off. Some of us went on to become well-known writers. And, perhaps most important, I found community in my new home.

WORKSHOP RULES

Charles Entrekin

What were we doing? As a cooperative, we were providing writing workshops, free and open to the public; we were providing a forum within the Berkeley community for the exchange of ideas, for criticism and support for the writing process; we were promoting poetry as a viable art form; we were publishing it, giving it the dignity of print; and we were having a say in what counts as literature in America.

We had grown into a successful cooperative because of a few informal rules we had adopted early on. For example, one of our rules was that in order to be printed in the *Berkley Poets Cooperative* magazine, poems had to be read and critiqued by the Co-op's editorial board. Another was that, at the Co-op meetings, everyone had the right to voice an opinion and that all opinions should be as honest as possible without being insulting. We asked the Co-op members to provide honest feedback: what were they getting out of the poem or story, what was it about, what worked or didn't work, what was praiseworthy and what was not. The Co-op was not a support group for weak egos. It was a writers' Co-op, and membership in it meant you were serious about your writing. It meant you were willing to hear people's honest opinions because you wanted to hear the truth about your work. Was it succeeding or failing? So it was expected that people should discuss the poem or story or piece of art as objectively as possible. There should be no ax-grinding. People should try to talk specifically about the poem or story. No one was allowed to attack a poem or story without a full explanation. Critiques had to be grounded in the work itself. No justifications by or for the author were allowed. The quality of the work was paramount. The poem had to be evaluated on its own, separate from the writer. So the critiques the writers were getting were as honest as we could make them. We were dedicated to the idea that we could build a Co-op of writers who were serious about writing, who were willing to learn and improve. And with that as our base, we felt we could go forward, publish good writers, and thereby have a say-so in our culture about what constitutes good writing and good literature.

This was a cooperative. Everyone had a voice, and no one could dominate. We wanted everyone to have an equal say and an opportunity to critique and a vote to accept or reject work. Then there had to be a majority vote. The cooperative was based on a constant insistence on the rules. We would periodically get people who wanted to change the rules, to change our focus, to promote different genres. Some wanted the Co-op to focus on feminist poetry, or working-class poetry, or language poetry, or concrete poetry. But we stayed firm in our eclecticism: a poem needed to be accepted or rejected on majority vote. We would print only the best work, regardless of form or subject matter.

We limited the editorial staff to ten people. Sometimes as few as five were on the staff, but we rotated the staff so that no one person or group could dominate. The staff would meet regularly and consider the submissions. People would argue and fight for the work they liked. It was a strong give and take as poets tried to persuade one another.

One of our best staff members was Bruce Hawkins. Bruce would constantly go through the reject pile and say that something did not deserve to be rejected, so it had to be reconsidered. He was an exceptional poet, thinker, and defender of the reject pile. He was also a decent basketball player, with a great long, outside shot. Below is my tribute to Bruce.

AT CODORNICES PARK
  for Bruce Hawkins
    poet and Sunday morning guard

And when pores open, legs pumping,
I see that his court awareness still survives,
a forty-year-old four-eyes who understands
this language of fast breaks and finger-tip
finesse, the backdoor pass and give and go,
and easy lay-ups.
    Because here is control
and that fun of full extension,
the face and flush of perfect
pick and roll. Because his hands
are filled with suggestions.
Because always his inscrutable sentences
begin in the arc of a hook shot.
    And the ball falls, spinning backwards
a prescribed imagistic route,
a will creating its own reasons
for grinning: sunlight, trees,
this irrevocable letting go
of what is already falling,
that sense of sweetest swish
thru unbroken string.

BERKELEY POETS COOPERATIVE/18

Bani-Sadr (left) listened as one of the militants spoke

1980

Contributors: Theresa Bacon, Dennis W. Folly, Philip Dacey, Hilda Johnston, Jane Rosenthal, Carla Kandinsky, John McKernan, Elaine Starkman, Rod Tulloss, Nancy Roxbury Knutson, Celestine Frost, Joe Sosensky, Claudia Chase, Stephen Beard, Lauren Liebling, Bruce Boston, Mark Taksa, Anne Cherner, Timothy Jacobs, Susan C. Strong, M.L. Hester, David Peniston, Kai Keya, Edward Decker, Stewart Florsheim, Diane Donovan, Don Skiles, Ramsay Bell, Ted Fleischman, Liz Socolow, S. Soloman, Virginia Elliot, Luke Wallin

Cover and artwork by Anthony Dubovsky

BPC Years: 1976–1988

A NEW WORLD OF WRITING

Carla Kandinsky

At a low point in my life, when I was a student at Contra Costa College, two members of the Berkeley Poets Cooperative gave a reading in Dorothy Bryant's creative writing class. I really wanted to go to the meetings they were describing, but I lived in San Pablo and had no way to get home at night from Berkeley. Determined to attend, I arranged to spend meeting nights at a friend's home on Ashby Avenue.

The group met at Charles Entrekin's house. I loved the very first meeting. Although I did enjoy being a student, the feeling of being in a roomful of writers was very different and exciting. I will never forget Jennifer Stone telling one poet that she should read her poem backward, starting with the last line and working her way up to the top. I was soon attending regularly and Wednesday night was the high point of my week. Perhaps "high" describes it because these people were high on writing and editing and publishing. In addition to the Berkeley Poets Cooperative magazine (which Bruce Hawkins was selling on the Berkeley streets), they were also publishing chapbooks of individual poets. I am writing "they" because at that time I felt I was simply an intrigued bystander, enjoying the group and appreciating the critique of my poetry. Later, I graduated to "we" and considered myself a member. For the first time, I had a chance to read my poetry to real live audiences. My first reading was at Contra Costa College with Bruce Boston. I believe he was reading from his chapbook *Jackbird*. It was really a great feeling being in front of the room, instead of seated at one of the desks. Before reading poetry, I had tried out for school plays every year in high school and never got a part because my voice was soft and I couldn't be heard. Poetry readings taught me the fine art of projecting over the noise of espresso machines, tabs being pulled off beer cans, and people unwrapping and eating sandwiches.

By 1976, I had moved into Berkeley with fiction and prose writer (and future ex-husband) Ralph Dranow. Frequently, Ralph and I did public readings together. At one time, I set a goal of doing one reading a month, not impossible, I found, as reading spaces were everywhere. I read at Cal State Hayward with Betty Coon from the Co-op, and someone had made a funny poster saying "Two Women Poets Riding in Tandem," with a picture of two women on a bicycle built for two. At that reading, I met Linda Kaplan, and we discovered we had the same birthday. Later, she called me, wanting to interview a woman poet for a class project. I remember telling her I was happy just reading in the East Bay and didn't care if I ever branched out. Little did I know then that in 1993 I would be the keynote speaker and teacher at the Alaska Women's Writing Conference at the University of Alaska, Anchorage. Linda and I became friends after the interview, and she began attending Co-op meetings. The first story of hers published in the Co-op magazine was "The Artichoke House," a story about communal living. Linda and I did many readings together, and she became a member of a writing group Ralph and I started at our apartment.

The '80s were an absolutely wild time for readings. There were readings every day and every night, in schools, bars, coffee shops, warehouses, and on the street. There was also grant money to pay poets to read to residents of assisted-living facilities. I was paid $10 per hour for these readings, and I traveled everywhere by bus, as far as San Leandro. I am now near the age to be a resident of one of these assisted-living homes, so my memory of exactly how some of these things came about is a little fuzzy.

In 1980, Ralph and I moved to Oakland, where writer Judy Wells and I became coordinators of a reading series at the Coffee Mill on Grand Avenue in Oakland. In 1982 and 1983, Judy and I were co-editors of *Woman Seed*, a publication that came out of a workshop at the Berkeley Women's Center. Judy and I ran the Coffee Mill reading series for two years. I had a rich field of readers to pick from, and many Berkeley Poet Co-op writers read there, including Lucy Day, Charles Entrekin, Ted Fleischman, Mark Taksa, Bruce Hawkins, Gail Rudd, Gerald Jorge Lee, and Linda Watanabe McFerrin.

I was privileged to be on the staff of the Co-op magazine, helping to select both poetry and fiction. And I was elated when in 1985 the Co-op published my chapbook, *Instead of a Camera*. I had been self-publishing little hand-sewn, Xeroxed books for several years, using drawings from art students and teachers to go with the poems. Many of them were about my life as an artist's model, and I called these books *The Nekkid Lady Series*. But *Camera* was a real book, with a real spine! Also in 1985, three poems were selected from the Co-op magazine for publication in *The Anthology of Magazine Verse, Yearbook of Poetry, 1985*. The three poems were "Golf" by Bruce Hawkins, "Afterword" by Gerald Jorge Lee, and my poem "Daddy."

Berkeley Poets Cooperative magazine's final issue was published in 1988. That was a sad day for all of the members, but changes were happening. Grant money was drying up, people were moving away. But all of us still carried valuable memories and lessons learned at the many meetings, editing sessions, and readings.

I have many literary milestones of which I am proud, but none of my achievements would have been possible without the encouragement I first found in the Co-op. Before I started going to meetings there, people would ask, "What do you do?" and I would say, "I'm a life-drawing model." After being a Co-op member, I would answer, "I'm a writer."

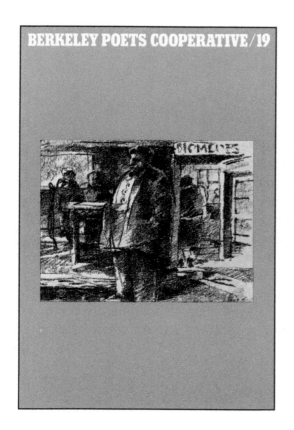

BERKELEY POETS COOPERATIVE / 19

1981

Contributors: Laura Conway, Dorien Ross, J.D. Woolery, A.J. Wright, Charles Entrekin, Bruce Nolan, Ron Schreiber, Ted Fleischman, Mark Taksa, Lucille Day, John Coveney, Christine Tollyfield, Tracey Kelly, C.S. Dawson, Hilda Johnston, John Krich, David Jaynes, Christine Zawadiwsky, Sharon Williams, Sarah Cotterill, Susan C. Strong, Ljiljana Bibovic, Carla Kandinsky, R.G. Koskovich, Diane Quintrall Lewis, Ramsay Bell, Nona Nimnicht, Bruce Hawkins, S. Solomon, Estelle Jelinek, Walter Cummins

Cover: Anthony Dubovsky
Artwork: Mike Lilly

A VERY SERIOUS VACATION

Michael Covino

In the late 1970's, I moved from New York to Berkeley to attend the Graduate School of Journalism at the University of California; and eventually, for some kind of much needed relief from that, I began attending the lively Wednesday night workshops of the Berkeley Poets Cooperative—sometimes as lively as an old Western barroom brawl—where I became a regular, satisfied customer. Indeed! To badly paraphrase another poet, to mangle him, journalism became my vocation and poetry became, if not my avocation, then, even better, my very serious vacation. And I am happy for that, and happy too for the friendships I made through the workshops—friendships that continue to this day, as does the writing of poetry. As does this lovely vacation.

BERKELEY POETS COOPERATIVE/20

1982

Contributors: Dennis Folly, Nellie Hill, Ramsay Bell Breslin, David Fisher, Bob Tomlinson, Lucille Day, Rofiah Breen, Doris Radin, Victoria Chames, Suzanne Finnamore, Deborah Linton, Charles Entrekin, Joan Boisclair, Mark Taksa, Susan Rawlins, Mark Antony Mastro, John McKernan, Carla Kandinsky, Crysta Casey, David Peniston, William Paul Yarrow, Michael Covino, Harold Witt, Ted Fleischman, Theresa Bacon, Dorian Ross, Judy Bebelaar, Michael Helm, Nancy Fleming Salz, Madeline T. Bass, Betsy Dubovsky, Oren J.J. Eisenberg, Gail Rudd, Bruce Boston, Beverly Silva, C.S. Dawson, Hilda Johnston, James Woolery, Sharon Williams, David Mitchell, Allan Morris

Cover: Anthony Dubovsky
Artwork: Mary Hayward

BPC Years: 1968–1991

1818 HEARST STREET

Charles Entrekin

In 1977, Maggie and I left Virginia Street and bought a bigger house, 1818 Hearst Street, close to University Avenue and the campus. It was a two-story classic box with a huge living room, big enough for the Berkeley Poets Workshop meetings. But, even so, most Wednesday night meetings, our living room was filled with poets, some driving down regularly from as far away as Napa Valley, new voices, poets from far and near. After Co-op meetings on Hearst Street, a large number of us would repair to fog-bound Brennan's Café, a sketchy late-night diner down by the Bay, for Irish coffees and beer, and sit around discussing the night's poems, the poetry scene, philosophy, and politics, until well after midnight.

Then in 1978, I resigned from Contra Costa College's Creative Writing program in order to focus on starting up a Creative Writing Program at John F. Kennedy University in Orinda. And for two years, I divided my energies between family, JFKU, the Berkeley Poets Cooperative, and my computer consulting work in San Francisco.

In 1980, the BPC celebrated its ten-year anniversary. As Fred Cody, of Cody's Bookstore, put it in his piece "The Bards of Berkeley": "Ten years strong, the Berkeley Poets Cooperative forges a significant alliance between writers and their community. [. . .] The new anthology by the Berkeley Poets Cooperative is a piece of a vision, a signpost to the future." (*Berkeley Monthly*, February 1981).

1983

Contributors: James Woolery, Gordon Grigsby, Christine Tollyfield, Bruce Hawkins, Rebecca Radner, Charles London Cyndian, Judy Silberman, Grace Bauer, Lucille Day, Jody Aliesan, Kathleen Lignell, Charles Entrekin, Julie Herrick White, Elaine Terranova, Suzanne Finnamore, Andy Whipple, Gail Rudd, Roger Bower, Rod Tulloss, Ralph Hunt, Tony D'Arpino, Mari Alschuler, Nina Tyksinski, Albert Huffstickler, Carla Kandinsky, Robert Bohm, Alice G. Brand, Neil Grill, John Oliver Simon, Larry Beresford, Ted Fleischman, Nancy Roxbury Knutson, Martin Steingesser, Rofiah Breen, Sidney Hollister, Teresa Mueller, Michael Moore, Paul Luchessa

Cover: Anthony Dubovsky
Artwork: Maggie Entrekin

BPC Years: 1978–1982

BLUE ARC

Ramsay Bell Breslin

I told Charles I wasn't going to contribute. So far I'd held fast.
But then, tonight, after reading a memorable account by a fellow
Co-op member of the BPC and BPW&P, my resolve cracked. Maybe
I could do it if I wrote about *now* instead of *then*. About how, when
asked to teach a one-day class to art student undergrads learning how
to put together a literary magazine, I had instinctively grabbed from
my bookshelf all the issues of the BPC that had either shaped me or
that I had helped shape from 1978 to 1982. As I sat around the table
learning the students' names, I leaned backwards in my chair until
I felt myself balanced on rear legs. This was a habit I'd formed in
high school to inject a small, personal risk into what I feared would
be a dull lesson. What caused me to knock my chair forward with
an embarrassing "bang" was the nearly simultaneous exclamation by
two students that they *loved* these magazines. Stupidly, defensively, I
assumed most of the students were political activist members of the
Occupy movement. As such, were they to stumble upon a poem of
mine in one of the magazines I'd brought, surely they'd be put off by
my poetic indictments of an unhappy childhood as too apolitical. "In
those days," I told them, "I was writing poems about dead baby birds."
Shortly thereafter, one young woman in the class nudged another and
pointed to a page in BPC Issue #20 (1982). Apparently, she'd found my
poem "Figuring," which concludes with me as a child standing in my
parent's driveway lifting the head of said bird. In life, I had wrapped
the little darling in Kleenex and buried it beneath the pine tree in our
backyard. It was this tree, taller than our house, I routinely climbed in
order to scare my mother into paying attention to me. For me, burying
the bird was the beginning of writing, which was the beginning of
looking, which was the beginning of looking at death.

No surprise then that I became an art writer whose business was
to look. Or that what I loved best about working on the BPC editorial
committee was the excitement of seeing Tony Dubovsky's latest cover

design. With each issue, the same format: a square frame within the slender rectangle of the front cover. In my era, the covers tended to be somber, serious, political. In BPC Issue #16 (1979), for example, a formalist photograph of a classical clay pot (shaped like an egg or dropped bomb) appears stamped onto an inky explosion above which it hovers, an objet d'art held apart from the history of a world at war. But by 1979, black body bags conveyed by American military planes no longer appeared on the evening news. By then America knew from atrocity photographs that in Cambodia under Pol Pot, simply killing a person had not been enough. We aspired to write political poems that didn't sound polemical; to forge a lyric with a saturnine edge.

I couldn't write that kind of poem. Instead, I tried to follow the lead of particular Co-op members whose poems inspired me by being recognizably their own. Theresa Bacon, Michael Covino, Lucy Day, Charles Entrekin, Dennis Folly, Rofiah Breen, Bruce Hawkins, Betsy Huebner, Ted Fleischman, Gail Rudd, Jo Ann Ugolini, Dorothy Wall, Sharon Williams, J. D. Woolery—these were among the names that mattered, because in those days, what mattered was "voice," what in the visual arts we once referred to as an artist's "signature style." When I pull up these roots to examine them, what I notice are the lines in my hands made visible by the dirt.

I refused the invitation to write about the Co-op because I felt I couldn't do justice to the complexity of my feelings. I still can't. But what I can do is document my role in the Co-op's history, as production person for Issue #18, art editor for Issue #19, and contributor to BPC Issues #15 through #20 and the *BPC Anthology*, in which poems of mine first appeared. As I write this, it is 2012, the year in which even non-readers have become aware that print culture is dying. At its heart, the Co-op was about books—even its magazine was a book—but it was also about the people who came together to share the poems they wrote, first with each other and then with the world. What made the Co-op successful was Charles's vision of what a poem could be. What made the Co-op strong were the arguments that broke out during workshops and at editorial meetings about what made a poem good. What made the Co-op last was Charles keeping steady the group's wild pulse without extinguishing its flame. After five years I left the Co-op to create a writing practice of my own.

BPC Years: 1978–1991

LATE NIGHT AT THE BERKELEY CO-OP

Mark Taksa

The floor creaks under your feet. Expectation
in voices makes the house young as first writing
found on an aged surface. Far from a sky
insistent of factory sugar and refinery oil, air consents.
You sit in a circle of people you know and do not know.

As if speaking from a shared mind, they invite
you to say your poem about the sea and a swimmer.
A woman's arm glides with the memory of water.
If you make the sea warm and over a gentle volcano,
she promises, she will swim deeper and longer.

The man who invents things of cold thought,
and so desires voices, has invited people from all streets.
He says the red hat need not float without intention
but could touch the swimmer like the caress of a lover.

The man who has sold many metaphors
says that the hat swaying in waves,
if one speaks as painter, is the dollop of paint
in a blue seascape that, swaying in waves,
makes us sway at life's openings.

Out the door, your eyes are salty with the late hour.
You carry the comments in your head, polishing
what you will say at the next meeting.
The street is too empty to tolerate more
than the whine of your ignition. No cars trouble the road...
So as not to wake your lover, you think of yourself
as a feather as you slide under the blanket.

BERKELEY POETS COOPERATIVE/22

1983

Contributors: Suzanne Finnamore, Betsy Dubovsky, James Woolery, Bruce Hawkins, John Campbell, Ralph Hunt, Martin Steingesser, Deborah Bruner, M.L. Hester, Al Ferber, Claudia Chase, Chrysta Casey, Sidney Hollister, Gerald Jorg Lee, Mark Taksa, Bruce Boston, Carla Kandinsky, Thelma Schwartz, Lyn Lifshin, Marguerite Judson Smith, Laurie Duesing, Hilda Johnston, Charles Entrekin, Teresa Bacon, Don Skiles, Nancy Rosbury Knutson, Gail Rudd, Ramsay Bell Breslin, Elise Morgan, Dennis Folly, David Herrstrom, Jaimee Wriston Colbert, Richard Grayson

Cover: Anthony Dubovsky
Artwork: Craig Schmitt

EVERY SITUATION IS A TEACHING

Tobey Kaplan

I look around…

"What took you to Berkeley?" some would ask. *I got in my car and drove/no invitations, no school, no job—just a few years late for the summer of love.*

When I was in my twenties, I had ambition and the Berkeley Poets Cooperative made me feel like I could make it; I knew many wonderfully talented and ambitious poets; I knew the Berkeley street personas, the independents, and academics…

I knew poetry was both solitary and cooperative— I immensely enjoy performing my work in front of a live audience.

And at that time—and still—poetry saves me—words won't fail me—I'm always writing—language nourishes. Poetry, perhaps all art, allows us to transform our disappointments and regrets. We accept the language and the good fortune that poetry has found us.

I met Charles at JFK University around 1978, after I had attended the old-school Creative Writing program at Syracuse University for my B.A. (1975) and just before the explosion of Associated Writing Programs and the M.F.A. approach to fame and recognition—and before I was accepted to the wonderfully amazing Interdisciplinary Studies in Creative Arts M.A. program at SF State!

In the summer of 1979, I went to Naropa and hung out with Ginsberg and his Buddhist boys—I began a writing retreat practice that led me to Bolinas—and Joanne Kyger—who is still a bust-ass poetry broad—and felt the legacy of Kerouac flow jump-cut rhythms through my NYC/SF cross-country bones.

Paul Simon was a Jewish kid who also went to high school in Queens—and that we share —that language has taken us into the common/shared rhythms of neighborhood/street/forest jungle village— where we connect with the ALL of human experience that is simultaneously lovely-dangerous, loaded with fear and risk—and demands that we embrace what we can of imagination.

The Poet in the World...

In the late '70s and '80s I was coming into my own voice as a community resource. As poet, one can be a shaman/sage/storyteller who enables folks to find their own voice in a society that makes it mute— a society that makes you need to shout—even if you have no idea how to speak or what to say.

And at the same time, I was working through California Poets in the Schools, as well as teaching creative writing through adult education at Contra Costa County Jail in Martinez, when this poem appeared in *Berkeley Poets Co-op #28*. It is a Berkeley poem that I love and have used quite a bit for teaching children third grade through high school:

WHAT DO YOU SEE?

The father says to his child in the stroller
they are out in the morning, it's hot
unusual very early; the child hears birds
and looks up to the trees for the source of sound.
There's a swatch of tape across his upper lip,
a delicate tube leading into his nostril
connected to a machine behind his stroller seat.

In that moment of sound and sight
the child is whole the father is fragile
as the air slips between them
the machine pumping uselessly
the voice that feeds the child sound
the wishful bird in flight
and warbling precious each breath
that the child makes, his father's morning
song in his chest
the color of rising sun.

This poem is what poetry is about—the art of paying attention and giving your eyes/heart to the moment and seeing where language takes you—

The Berkeley Poets Cooperative served as the community where you could come and go—you were embraced, you were accepted; people that I knew from all sectors of the poetry community, and those I still run into, showed up at readings and workshops—

Charles and company made it comfortable and family—where lots of us made friends or found old friends (Stewart Florsheim and I met as undergrads at Syracuse University) and we still see one another and remain dedicated to the rhythm of the line/the word/the verse—the primacy of imaginative language and how it enriches and continues to enlarge our experience and our world and connects us to one another . . .

The Berkeley Poets Cooperative was our gathering place, the commons, a living room: a family of drifters/hipsters/would-be academics where you could read your poems get some nods—get some feedback, feel respected. Some went on to other things literary—others went on to varying degrees of recognition and approval—while the voices of still others shifted and continue to drift and shift in the attics and basements and second hand bookshops that might still exist throughout our digital paperless landscape (I have promised my students—kindergarten through college—that I would plant a forest because of all the paper I have consumed.)

Bridge Over Troubled Waters . . .

A song that's about relationship where someone symbolically lays down one's body to bring a friend/a lover through difficult times; where the crisis inspires action and makes the other person central in one's life. Relationship is the essence of change. As a poet and teacher, I encourage my students to embrace the challenge change brings.

I'm a poet/community activist/artist who doesn't usually have scholarly pretensions, but I've been a teacher for thirty years, working to empower both adults and children through their own curiosity with language and ideas and images. I haven't promoted my own work, but it is immensely challenging—creative and rewarding. Today I work as a mentor for Native Americans and assist children and adults, identifying skills and talents and finding a way through the user-unfriendly education system—so they can survive spiritually and creatively. That's the most important element of education, in my view—to feel confident about one's questions and to love one's own curiosity. My years as a Berkeley poet involved with other poets allowed me all of this.

I build a bridge out of my approach to teaching as a poet in the world—based on developing students' habits of the mind and their trust in their own experience—where the words originate, letting the words take them over.

The Buddhists say *everyone is a teacher; every situation is a teaching*—perhaps all we need to do is cultivate those habits of mind, practice, and patience to make it so.

BPC Years: 1978–1980

ALIEN TALK, OR, HOW THE BERKELEY POETS CO-OP SAVED MY LIFE

Nina Burghild Holzer

It must have been around 1978 that I first came to the Berkeley Poets Co-op, and it was a crucial turning point in my life. My life was in crisis on every conceivable level, and my life as a writer was in question as I faced one identity crisis after another, along with the political and social turmoil of the time.

I was an immigrant who had come to America on a one-year student visa in 1964, and by now, some fourteen years later, had fought myself through layers and layers of cultural and economic and bureaucratic obstacles, as immigrants do, and was now living in San Francisco as a legal permanent resident with an "alien registration card." I had recently gone through divorce proceedings and had, in the years before this time, left a Ph.D. program in Literature at UC San Diego, because the department was disintegrating with political in-fights and there was no faculty left that could help me with my dissertation. After that, I then returned to Europe to help my family through their own crises, and had discovered that re-integrating into Austrian cultural and academic life was simply not feasible. I then came back to San Francisco and to my "Alma Mater" San Francisco State, where my journey as a "foreign student" had begun. In 1977, I enrolled in the master's program for creative writing at San Francisco State University and was finally doing what I always wanted to do—writing, for real!

One would think that I had finally arrived on solid ground, but nothing was further from the truth; what I experienced at that time was extreme alienation. The years of my fractured identities as an immigrant had finally caught up with me and were haunting me. And the place where this battle took place was the realm of language. Language is literally a writer's lifeline. As long as you have the words to express what you are experiencing, you can survive almost anything; in fact you can heal, because the very act of artistic creation is whole-making. But what if your language fails you, what if it splinters into multi-lingual, multi-cultural fragments, a heap of tiny mosaic stones, each laden with sensory significance for yourself, but making little sense to anyone else? What if you fail to put the fragments together, into one whole image, into a reality comprehensible in a particular culture, language, or environment? That's where I was at that time in my life—end of the line, a bilingual writer who couldn't write a sensible paragraph of prose in either language, a student who refused to write even one line of "expository" anything, and an ex-graduate assistant and Ph.D. candidate who never wanted to explain a piece of literature to anyone ever again, least of all her own writing.

And that's where poetry came in! You can say a lot with very little, you can hide layers and layers of pain in one tiny metaphor, you can make multilingual sounds, you can hint and hint and hint with small gestures at huge realities, and you can use broken fragments of identity and create an odd composition that somehow is a whole something after all. I should say that my battles with language at that time didn't have much to do with the fact that English was my second language. I had grown up speaking German, but I had learned English early in life, had spent some time in England, and was fluent by the time I came to America. I experienced an enormous sense of freedom when I first began to write in English, and I embraced this language like a lover and never let go of it. But like many artists, I discovered later that the sounds of your mother tongue, and all the sensory experiences we have in our childhood, are like the basic elements that later nourish our creative process, but they are very resistant to translation, both to verbal and cultural translation.

Even within a particular country and language, one can experience great shifts in one's experienced reality that are difficult to "translate" when one moves, for instance, from one landscape or social environment to another, or when there are sudden political or cultural changes sweeping through an entire generation. I had come to America, and to the San Francisco Bay Area, at exactly such a time of change and had found this exhilarating when I was a young student. There was the Free Speech Movement, and the Civil Rights Movement, and the protest against the Vietnam War, and against all wars. There was the Women's Movement and the Movement for the Rights of

Minorities, the Farm Labor Movement, the Environmental Movement, and many other just and good causes. But as wave after wave of these changes swept through all our personal lives over the next decades, there was, for me, also a numbness and exhaustion that set in. For an immigrant, who has to shift through enormous changes in identity and at the same time fight to survive and succeed in a new environment, which itself is changing over and over, there comes a point where there is too much loss—of home, of family, of belonging, and connection—and there is no grounding, no language left to express that bottomless reality. For a writer this can be a life threatening situation, and it was so for me. I felt that the poetry I was writing at that time was my last lifeline, and my enrollment in the Creative Writing Program at San Francisco State was a desperate attempt to come home somehow. But it wasn't working very well. For one I was resisting being a student again, tired of sitting in classes that I could have been teaching. And San Francisco was as cold and foggy and lonely as it had always been—a difficult place to call home.

And this is where the Berkeley Poets Co-op comes in! And a poem entitled "Alien Talk" became the key to a new opening. I had begun to write a collection of poems later entitled *Fragments of the Geranium Woman,* and "Alien Talk" was one of the first bilingual poems I had written that attempted to portray the inner life of an immigrant, with voices speaking in different languages. I was sitting in the empty classroom at San Francisco State, and had just listened to my fellow students as they shredded my poem, obviously not knowing what to do with it. As they all walked out, and I sat there, contemplating whether to destroy the poem or myself, or both, a young man walked up and began to chat with me about writing poetry and about the Berkeley Poets Co-op, where anyone could come and read their poems. He seemed a bit like an angel at the time, sent miraculously to save me in my despair, or at least that's how I told the story later on; I really can't recall the exact sequence of events. This person was Stewart Florsheim, who later became a very good friend and fellow Poets Co-op member. It probably took him a few times to talk me into coming, because I was not eager to join any group, much less have my poems "discussed." But when I finally did come, I brought my poem "Alien Talk" and they listened with great care, they asked questions, they gave technical suggestions on how to deal with the language barriers that came up in multilingual texts, and so forth. There was cooperation, not competition. I knew that I had found a group of fellow writers, equals, and a family of sorts.

The BPC had a great variety of writers that came and went, people of all ages and walks of life. The workshop groups were usually small; we met at each other's homes, mostly in Berkeley; some people came from across the Bay, as I did. Several members were also students of the Creative Writing Program at San Francisco State, and for a while we formed a little sub-group, hung out with each other in the halls or cafeteria or at the Poetry Center upstairs. We swapped manuscripts and gave each other feedback before submitting our work to teachers and publishers. Some of us stayed friends for many years after that, worked on translation projects together, or gave readings together. Stewart Florsheim and Laura Schiff and I translated various German poets into English and had a great time meeting and fighting and gossiping, and eating good food while we did all this. A core group at the BPC participated more closely in the production of the magazines and chapbooks that the BPC published. I was not so involved in that, but could always be counted on to give good feedback on anyone's work and for years, long after many of us had moved away, we still sent each other our manuscripts or newest publications.

I was an active member of the BPC for about two or three years. In the months after I attended my first meeting, my poem "Alien Talk" was published in the latest BPC magazine, and it was later also included in the anthology *The Best of the Berkeley Poets Cooperative*. I graduated from San Francisco State University with a master's degree in art and submitted a creative thesis that consisted entirely of bilingual poetry. "Alien Talk" was of course included. As I put the collection *Fragments of the Geranium Woman* together, I contemplated the fact that I didn't feel "alien" anymore. The fragments of my life had somehow come together and formed a mosaic portrait in my written work. And I had become part of a large network of artists and writers that extended all over the Bay Area and beyond. In the following fall semester, SF State University hired me to teach in the Creative Writing Department. I became a mentor to all the multilingual and multicultural students who desperately wanted to write, but didn't know how to put their fragmented stories together.

In the summer of 1979 I moved from the foggy City to a little sunny farm near Morgan Hill, about 70 miles south of San Francisco. I commuted in to teach twice a week, and to attend occasional readings and BPC meetings. The rest of the time I lived the glorious life of a country writer and helped in the vineyards of a nearby winery. I was not isolated. Artists and writers came from the city and loved to visit my little country retreat. A large group from the Berkeley Poets Co-op came for a rare out-of-town get-together, bringing kids and significant others, baskets of food and wine. I don't think we got much work done that day, but we made a beautiful photograph of the entire group, all standing on my grape-vined porch and obviously having a good time. I lived in this house for four years before the winds of change blew hard again and I had to move.

I stopped writing poetry and began to write journals and tell stories. Helping other people tell their difficult life stories became my life's work. I created radio programs, taught workshops, collected stories from those who had no public voice. In 1999, I finally left the Bay Area and moved to the Klamath River in northernmost California. I moved to be with the Native people there because I wanted to hear their stories and learn their songs. And I am still here.

1984

Contributors: Ralph Hunt, Sydney Hollister, Bruce Hawkins, James Sutherland-Smith, Robert Frazier, Gail Rudd, Martha Wolfe, Barbara Nilsson, Nina Tyksinski, Suzanne Finnamore, Paul M. Strohm, Diana Blackmon, Carol Ann Russell, Alicia Ostriker, Lyn Lifshin, Carla Kandinsky, Charles V. Olynyk, Gerald Jorge Lee, Albert Huffstickler, Charles Entrekin, G.P. Guillermo, Beverly Lauderdale, Arthur Dembling

Cover: Anthony Dubovsky
Artwork: Kelly Finnerty

BPC Years: 1968–1991

SONOMA STREET AND 2642 DANA STREET

Charles Entrekin

During the 1980s, there were big changes in my life. With three partners, I founded a computer consulting company, The Application Group, Inc. At a poetry reading at Noe Books & News, I met and subsequently fell in love with poet Virginia Gail Rudd, now Gail Rudd Entrekin. In the midst of confusion and heartbreak, I got divorced, remarried, gained a stepson, Ben, had another son, Nathan, and then a daughter, Katy, and then, with Demian and Caleb, we were five.

In 1984, for a short while, Gail and I moved into a rental on Sonoma Street in Berkeley and held a year's worth of BPC meetings, publishing two chapbooks and Issues #23, #24, #25, and #26. Then, in 1986, Gail and I bought a grand old Craftsman style house on the edgy side of south Berkeley, 2642 Dana Street, one block off of the ever vibrant Telegraph Avenue. Over the next six years, we published Co-op magazine issues #27, #28, #29, #30, and six chapbooks, concluding in 1990 with *The Impossibility of Redemption Is Something We Hadn't Figured On* by Linda Watanabe McFerrin and Chitra Divakaruni's *The Reason for Nasturtiums*.

BERKELEY POETS COOPERATIVE/24

1984

Rod Tulloss, Sonia Saxon, Michael Koch, Mark Taksa, Grace Wade Grafton,
Bill Yarrow, Bruce Boston, Beverly Silva, Carla Kandinsky, Susan Kolodny,
Martin Steingesser, Charles Entrekin, Gail Rudd, Elise Morgan, Theresa Bacon,
Nina Tyksinski, Sidney Hollister, Nancy Roxbury Knutson, Nona Nimnicht,
Shane Doheny, Gerald Jorge Lee, J.D. Woolery, Karen Kevorkian, Mary Louise
Hill, Allan Morris

Cover: Anthony Dubovsky
Artwork: Edie Scott Hoffman

THE TIME OF OUR LIVES

Gail Rudd Entrekin

To talk about the Berkeley Poets Workshop & Press is to talk about my husband, Charles Entrekin. By the time I came to the Co-op in 1981, he had, for twelve years, been the driving force behind its theory and practice, as well as its host. So to be caught up in the work of the Co-op was always, whether we knew it or not, to be caught up, to one extent or another, in Charles's vision of what poetry can be, what it can do. Of how we should go about making a poem all that it intends to be.

I came to California with friends, having just finished an M.A. degree in English literature with a concentration in poetry from Ohio State University, and I came to the poetry Mecca, San Francisco, to be among the poets I most admired. I was 30 when I arrived, and for a couple of years I worked as an editor and technical writer before my mother came across an article about BPW&P from the *New York Times*, which had been reprinted in the Cleveland *Plain Dealer*, and sent it my way.

I was running a poetry reading series at my friend Edie's book store, Noe Books & News, on Market Street in San Francisco. Someone gave me his number and I called up Charles Entrekin, one of the poets in the newspaper article, and invited him to bring a few other members of the Co-op across the Bay to read. They gave a great reading (even allowing for the disgruntled Karen Brodine, who was, I discovered, a radical pro-union activist. When I explained that the take at the door didn't even cover the wine, so we couldn't afford to pay the poets, she shouted that we were failing to respect the rights of the worker. I was stunned. After that Edie and I often split the cost of the wine out of our own pockets and offered the poets the door receipts.)

A few months later, I drove across the bridge to Berkeley, which felt like another country, to the grey-blue house on Hearst Street. The group that night was quite intimidating. I had met Karen, Susan and Dick Strong, Charles, Bruce Hawkins, and Bruce Boston at the book store reading, and they had been pleasant, if distant. There were few women in the hierarchy of the Co-op at that time, and it soon seemed to me that the three-man core of Charles and the two Bruces had not thought about trying to provide a kind of social fabric.

There were few pleasantries and no one explained how things were done. It took me months to figure out that there was a magazine and that it was produced by a panel of editors who self-selected from the group as they began to absorb the system. As a co-op, by definition, no one was in charge, though everyone knew that Charles, with his gentle, quiet Southern way, was the de facto leader.

People at Co-op meetings were outspoken. They were neither friendly nor unfriendly. It was just about the work. The men especially seemed unaware that their comments might elicit emotional reactions and were completely focused on the work itself. It felt a bit dangerous . . . grad school workshops and critiques had been carefully kind, by comparison. But there was an element of relief in being among people who were truly disinterested and who were so wholly dedicated to working out the puzzle of each poem.

Occasionally someone was excessively critical. Once, Ramsay Bell (Breslin) said to me, after I had offered a badly expressed criticism, "You don't know much but you know what you like, huh, Gail?" I saw later that she was only teasing me with a phrase that was popular at the time, but the fact that it has stuck with me all these years is a testament to its sting.

But Charles, for one, was ever kind, ever careful. He almost always spoke last and, over the years, it always seemed to me that he was invariably the person in the room who most often spoke rightly about the *concept* of the poem, the shape the poem was striving to take. He was very focused on the music of poems and his intuition was, for me and for many others over the years, formidable. I felt, and still feel, that he was the best critic of poetry I ever knew.

Charles had studied under Richard Hugo, whom I had never heard of till Charles gave me *The Lady in Kicking Horse Reservoir*. Charles believed, as I did, with Gerard Manley Hopkins, that each poem is struggling to inhabit its own true shape. Charles taught that our job as critique-ers of a poem was to help the poet achieve her/his true intention. Never to judge that intention. Never to judge the person.

Our job was to immerse ourselves in the poem and to recognize where it was running off its natural course. In truth, I think he may have been unaware of how few people are *able* to do this, how most of us simply lack this facility. Or at least are unable to bring it to bear at will. For him it was almost a meditation. While the rest of us were working out the misplaced commas and the inconsistent tenses, while the new people were arguing with the *message* of the poem, while people were hotly debating whether or not the poet had his/her information right, Charles was largely quiet, letting the poem simmer somewhere on a burner outside of conscious control.

And then, so often when he spoke, it was to say something so unexpected, non-linear, something so right and clear that none of us had realized, something that lit the poem and made it whole. He moved a stanza. He pointed out where the music had been violated. He suggested a new way to *focus* the poem all together, to set it on a truer course. While the rest of us patted and poked, he lifted the poem whole from the oven and gave us a vision of how delicious it could be. This is how it seemed to me.

I learned from Charles, over the years, how to wait and let the thing stew. Eventually, I stopped being the first one to speak, stopped rushing in with my first thought, and learned to wait, to think again. He taught me to slow down and roll the thing around in my mouth. I learned to watch for what he called "something at stake" in the poem. We talked about what I remembered from grad school of T.S. Eliot's "objective correlative," attaching the emotional thread of the poem to something from objective reality...something for the reader to hold on to, to get oriented by.

We talked about Wordsworth's belief that poetry is the "overflow of powerful emotion recollected in tranquility" and the importance of waiting for that tranquility to arrive. I shared his aversion to political diatribe and to personification that challenges credibility and to the easy rhyme. We talked about not setting out with intent to say this or that in the poem, as one would do in an essay, but rather to plunge in, make space for it, and allow the poem to come to you. We talked about how his past experiences with hallucinogenic drugs allowed him to let go in that way while a poem was coming to him...more easily than I with my need to control the thing from start to finish.

We talked about the need for revision, the importance of understanding that the poem is never really finished. That "getting" a finished poem should never really be the goal, but rather the process itself is the goal and the poem is evidence of the level of purity of that process. (Though I had a hand in articulating this long-held perspective of Charles's, I have really never been able to fully embrace it. I do so like a nice end product, all tidied up and ready to sally forth into the world.)

We developed a shared reality about poetry over the years, so that we came to swim in the same pool of words: quotes and who said them and where and why, what a given phrase represents to us, a large, often complex series of discussions over many years, all fronted by a few simple words. We found we both knew Dylan Thomas by heart (He: "When I was a windy boy and a bit/and the black spit of the chapel fold..." I: "When I was young and easy under the apple boughs/about the lilting house and happy as the grass was green...") We both knew dozens of poems and random lines and we took the lines apart and found where even the great poets could have used a good critiquing group.

Once we were together, the Co-op was an integral part of our life. We planned for it, wrote for it, spent hours talking about the poems we heard there. Our own emotional lives materialized on the page like Polaroid prints, and we pored over each other's lines as well as our own for clues to who we were and how we felt. We lay on our backs murmuring and declaiming in our shared language into the sky.

Meanwhile, I attempted to make the meetings more welcoming and the Press's workings more clear. I made friends who came and stayed for a long while or a short while and later went away. People were spontaneously kind. Bruce and Ann Hawkins welcomed me into Charles's life when others stood back uncertainly. Carla Kandinsky took off her earrings and gave them to me after I admired them. Tobey Kaplan let me follow her around, training to teach for California Poets in the Schools, which I did for many years. And Chitra Divakaruni put in a word for me with the hiring committee at Diablo Valley College, my first teaching job, which led to 25 years of college teaching. Linda McFerrin and I shared a few sad and many happy times together (including reciting "Fern Hill" together in a hot tub!).

Too, there were a few questionable spontaneous acts over the years: the drunken theft of our wind chime from our front porch after a meeting on Sonoma Street and another member shooting beer all over our living room walls. Someone took our pot plants on Dana Street and several people called Charles, drunk and sober, for advice in the middle of the night.

Pregnant with our son Nate, my water broke and I went into labor during a Co-op meeting in 1986, and everyone went home as we left for the hospital. Many kind gifts and wishes followed.

Charles would come in from work, his tie hanging like a noose, and the little kids would run to jump on him. We would eat a hurried dinner, the older boys would go out to friends or to their rooms to study, and we would get the little ones down in time for the Co-op meeting. Sometimes a baby cried upstairs or a kid padded downstairs in footed pajamas, and I had to excuse myself. Members were ever patient.

The Berkeley Poets Co-op and all that came with it was one of the dominant colors woven into the fabric of our life.

BERKELEY POETS COOPERATIVE/25

1985

Contributors: Carol Adler, Charles Entrekin, Nina Tyksinski, Deborah Schupack, W.L. Gertz, Philip Sean Brady, Loss Pequeño Glazier, Theresa Bacon, Gerald Jorge Lee, Chris King, Carla Kandinsky, Stewart Florsheim, Rebecca Radner, Edwin Drummond, Edward Goldman, Rusane Morrison, Charles London Cyndian, Sonia Saxon, Bonnie Roberts, James Russell Williams, Jan McCann, Georgia Johnston, Bruce Hawkins, Neil Grill, J.D. Woolery, Art Homer, Lyn Lifshin, Gail Rudd, Bruce Boston, Jody Scott

Cover and Artwork: Ross Drago

BPC Years: 1984–1990

THE END OF THE CO-OP

Marilee Richards

I became interested in poetry, don't ask me why, in my late thirties, about 1984. No background in literature or writing. I started with a few evening classes, one with Rafael Gonzales, one with Richard Silberg, on "Appreciating and Writing Contemporary Poetry," a couple of others. After Richard Silberg's class, I asked him, "What should I do now?" He suggested I go to the Berkeley Poets Co-op, which I had never heard of. He said to me (I don't know why I remember this), "Charles left his woman," in a solemn but also gossipy way, as if talking about a movie star or prominent politician. Who was Charles? I didn't know.

I don't remember how I found my way to my first Co-op workshop. A few people were gathered in a living room in a house in the hills of Berkeley. Charles and Gail were obviously very much together. I thought, "Richard Silberg doesn't know what he's talking about." It was a while before it became clear, partly from the poems they were sharing, that Charles had indeed just left his wife and that he and Gail *were* a brand new couple.

> I know you are going to
> take her
> in the morning
> when you leave our bed
> disappear down in your silver car.
> She will be hollow, brittle, clean.
> She will lean
> and you will be wearing your strength.
> Her hand in yours
> you will answer for her
> calmly, she will let go completely;
> you are taking care . . .

—From *"On the Occasion of the Wife's Abortion, the Mistress Speaks" by Gail Entrekin*

For months, I thought the Co-op was just a place where you came to get feedback on poems. Shy by nature, especially in groups, it was all I could do to make myself walk through that front door every couple of weeks, beginner's poem in hand, and face the comments, tactful as they usually were. One evening, a couple of unfamiliar guys came in carrying boxes full of that season's Co-op magazine. That is how I found out about the Co-op's publication side.

Berkeley itself, as a place, idea, or symbol, was never especially important to me. Although I was brought up pretty conventionally in the conventional fifties, it was in a family without dogma, so I never had much to rebel against and also never developed much interest in politics or current events. Although I am a descendent of the earliest Utah Mormon pioneers, my particular branch of the family was at first doubting, then skeptical, then rebellious toward Church doctrine and ended up doing the unheard-of in a tiny Mormon town, leaving the Church. My religious education was confined to *Mormon beliefs are ridiculous. Don't you ever join the Church.* Fortunately, my polygamist-Mormon-ranching background has provided a lot of unique material to mine for poems:

> The ladies bring apricot jam
> to the door as if mere preserves could lure
> my grandmother back to church.
> The end is at hand. Tithe
> and be saved. The flowered one
> laughs absently. Lottie in polka dots
> follows her lead. Tears slide
> down a pitcher of lemonade. Earthquakes.
> Drought. The fields of the Gentiles,
> their animals blighted by plague,
> babies dropping like soft-boiled eggs
> off the continent's ragged edge...

—*From "The Ladies" by me*

I also tended to be inward and solitary and would never have been enticed by crowds, marches, and confrontations. From my very earliest years, I was drawn to nature and the outdoors. While Berkeley was fomenting with free speech, anti-war, and farm labor demonstrations, I jogged around Lake Merritt, bicycled country roads, and backpacked most of the trails in the northern Sierra, then got married, had two boys and settled into a child welfare job with Alameda County. . . . Boooorrriing. . . . Berkeley and the Co-op in the years when the Co-op was just getting started and Berkeley was still at the height of its activism must have been very exciting places, but. . . I missed out.

Once I began attending the Co-op workshops, I made sure I always had a poem to present. This meant writing a couple of poems a month. I was always envious when Carla Kandinsky flew through the door with a perfectly crafted poem she had just scribbled on an envelope while riding the bus. It took me hours and hours and dozens of revisions to come up with a poem I was even remotely satisfied with. Writing was, for me, unpleasant and never easy. I think I stuck with it only because it felt so magical when those few words actually came together and worked. Also, Charles was, from the first, gently but obviously encouraging. He seemed to see a potential, way before anything of interest actually began happening on paper. I have always felt deeply grateful to him for this.

GIVE ME A BREAK

Some poets spend eight years in
a Buddhist monastery — no heat,
no lights, hours of meditation.
During this time – no writing.
I want to be in love, a year,
seven years, a lifetime, however
long it takes. So don't ask me
to write, I'm studying joy, I'm
learning to meditate on the body
of a man. I want to worship him
with apricots and kisses. I'm
happy, I'm sorry, I have nothing
more to say.

—by Carla Kandinsky (probably written on the bus)

At some point, I came across *The Writer's Market* and then *Poets & Writers Magazine* and began sending out. I had immediate beginner's luck with two poems accepted by *The Southern Review*. Over the next few years I had several dozen poems, almost everything I wrote, accepted and printed in many of the good literary journals of the day. I was selected for an award of $2,500 by the California Arts Council, and some journal or other, I can't remember which, nominated a poem for a Pushcart Prize, which I didn't get. I was a finalist in a couple of the bigger First Book contests. I also had a sense of starting to become just a tiny bit "familiar" to a few names in the wider poetry world. During this time, I also had a couple of poems published in the Co-op magazine and helped work on one of the last published issues.

I don't know how Charles started the Co-op or how it became something of a force. I never even really figured out how it was structured. By the time I came on board, about 1985, the exciting times as I have imagined them (a mangled frenzy of bongo drums and soft drugs along with the barefoot, topless poetics) were pretty much over. The first year or so that I attended, the meetings attracted a dozen or more with a wider variety of people dropping in. Charles and Gail moved a couple of times, eventually settling into a house on a leafy street off Telegraph. Every other Wednesday, I walked through their gate, greeted the German shepherd on the porch, and settled in for three hours. Sometimes Charles was just getting home himself, taking off his hat and coat and looking tired. The babies had been put away. Gail had a pot of tea on the stove. By then, only five or six other people were showing up, pretty much regulars. It wasn't a warm lovey-dovey group by any means. Friendly in only a polite, distant way. Didn't seem to matter how many times we sat together in the cozy living room around the big coffee table; cordial was as close as we got. But the feedback was excellent. You knew what these people were giving you was honest and valuable. And free. You could pay attention and improve...or not. I presented my poem and listened to the comments. I don't think I could have done better at any M.F.A. workshop.

One evening, when it was my poem being discussed, Jaimes sniffed *clever writing*. I was pleased. Yes, it *was* clever writing. I had managed to grab on to the style of the day and was running with it to the literary journals. But *Clever* often hangs out with its friends, *Shallow* and

Distant. Jaimes wrote barely more than a dozen poems which he later gathered together in a thin volume he titled *Small Lies*. They are honest and ragged and elegant. I have developed a far greater appreciation of transparency, openness and authenticity in writing, although I am still often seduced by *Clever's* lopsided grin.

> The small lies we make for ourselves
> to get us by, to see us through the day
> stay with us long past the reason for them
> and there will always be someone close
> to expose us over dinner
> in the company of strangers
> when there is nothing even
> to be gained by it anymore
> but the moment's width and satisfaction,
> the personal and reminding shame. . .

—From Small Lies *by Jaimes Alsop*

I also continued to take other classes and to read gobs of poetry on my own. During those years, independent bookstores were still plentiful and actually had roomy poetry sections. You could duck into Cody's and find the latest issue of *Ploughshares*, *The American Poetry Review,* or an author in the Pitt Poetry Series. At a writer's conference in Aspen, I attended a workshop taught by Bin Ramke and got his particular slant on poetry. But the Co-op was always my mainstay.

Sometime in the early nineties, Charles and Gail moved on with their lives and moved away. The Co-op was a ghost of its former self by then anyway, the magazine defunct, only a very few of us coming regularly to the Wednesday workshops. Once there were no more meetings, I could no longer write poems. I was the grandfather clock whose old man had died. I tried, but it was hopeless. Obviously, with no poems to send out, that was the end of my journal publication as well. The daily struggles to strangle a decent line into being, the meetings, the sending out, the acceptance and rejection notices, the contributor's copies arriving in the mail, the teeny tiny bits of recognition—all a big part of my life for years, just gone.

Other things eventually filled in, I suppose. In 2005, the Entrekins called me about putting out a book and a few months later *A Common Ancestor* was published. That was great. Having a real book made me feel more like a real poet and has given me credibility.

In 2001, my husband and I followed through on a longtime plan. I retired from interviewing adoptive parents at the County, and he found a job at a boarding school in Sedona. We sold our house in Alameda and moved to be closer to The Great Wild Outdoors.

It takes actually living in a place to learn its true nature. In Arizona, you don't mess with a person's Freedoms. Which here means. . . guns. I haven't noticed much concern over, say, the freedom to not be hassled for being brown. In California I never stood next to some cowboy-in-his-own-mind with a holstered gun standing in line at the grocery store. Or the bank. Guns are allowed anywhere, unless a sign is posted outside saying otherwise. In Arizona, Stranger, we aim to be prepared, just in case a gang of rustlers rides into town.

Sedona itself, other than its landscape, has little sense of place. It basically popped into existence only in the last few decades, as elderly white people (like ourselves) noticed it was a sunny and spectacular place to retire. The colorful, eclectic mass of humanity, as it exists in the Bay Area that keeps you on your toes, just bobbing and weaving and making allowances, is absent. Having only our own kind for company, we become brittle and suspicious.

For a few years, I cast about looking for some meaningful way to fill my days, now void of both a full time job and kids. I volunteered at the library and at the local hospice, took long hikes with the dog, even tried out more involved dinner recipes. I became a newly minted senior Happy Homemaker. My elderly mother moved in. But I was, nevertheless, without a real sense of purpose or identity.

Finally, one day in 2006, I got it into my head to somehow find a way to teach a poetry class. What made me think I could do this with my quiet personality, no teaching experience, no M.F.A., and no place to start, I have no idea. But the recipes weren't doing it for me. I went to the local arts center, which occasionally listed a writing class among all the painting classes, but the director didn't think I could spark enough interest. A friend then told me about OLLIE, the newly established Osher Life Long Learning Center, basically for older people.

You didn't need any particular credentials to teach there, only the interest of other people willing to go to your class. I got a dozen sign-ups for my first class, which I patterned after the class I had taken with Richard Silberg.

Amazingly, my classes started off well and kept perking right along. Then, about the fourth meeting while we were discussing a poem titled "Desire" by Stephen Dobyns, a woman in her thirties who had obviously been to one too many women's studies classes, walked out, declaring the poem to be misogynistic. Just a few minutes later, little ninety-two year old Amelia raised her hand and wanted to know just how long a man's orgasm lasted anyway. *Uh, how about you check with Ed on that one, Amelia.* Now, moving on to the next poem...

I've been teaching classes there ever since. Facilitating is a more accurate word. I love my fellow learners who are brilliant and educated and talented and funny and always willing to try something new. This has happened several times: a newish poet struggles and struggles and then suddenly—*Oh, My God, out of seeming nowhere a Poetic Diamond. Someone get the World on the phone!* I find this very exciting, but...life here *is* pretty slow.

YESTERDAY

Yesterday
I lost another game
of conversational ping pong, thinking
I was this time prepared,
strategy planned, sure
to win the game. Forgot

he hits out of my range,
fast and sure,
prepared, annoyingly accurate.

Silence between us,
a shut-out match.

—*by Dee Popat*

In addition to regular writing classes, I also have a goofy class now called Poetry Hikes. My co-leader, the world's most outgoing retired physicist, Gary, leads our group to a spectacular spot in the Sedona red rocks, where I hand out a poem to be read and discussed. We analyzed "The Emperor of Ice Cream" on Coffee Pot Rock, of Folger's Coffee commercial fame, on a spectacular morning in April. The group, mostly new to poetry, dove right in. What is *a dresser of deal* anyway? Whose horny feet are protruding? What are those things on the sheet? What is this really about? This class gets a little bigger each season. I also have a workshop of a few writers, gleaned from my classes, which meets a couple of times a month. We may not be as advanced as the old Co-op group, but we *are* family. With a workshop again in place, I have been able to write a few new poems. Without the Co-op, my interest in poetry and very modest success would never have been sustained past those first evening classes. Especially in view of the steady accumulation of losses and failings plaguing these later decades in one way or another for all of us, I'm grateful that poetry has been a part of my life and to be able to pass on to others the kind of support that the Co-op once provided to me.

LOSING THE LIGHT

It's as if you've been thrown
like a stone
across moments, bouncing
only from surface tension,
knowing you are losing
the here and now,
the world still outside
all around you,
an ordinary day.

—*From* Listening: New and Selected Work *by Charles Entrekin*

BERKELEY POETS COOPERATIVE/26

1985

Alicia Ostriker, Robert Frazier, Susan Kolodny, Deborah Bruner, Mark Taksa, James Cushing, Carla Kandinsky, Ivan Arguelles, Thomas Wiloch, Philip Brady, Grace Bauer, Lyn Lifshin, Theresa Bacon, S.A. Robbins, Crysta Casey, James Sutherland-Smith, Bruce Boston, Fritz Hamilton, J.D. Woolery, Gail Rudd, Bruce Hawkins, Lucie Work, Lucille Day, Tony D'Arpino, Carol Cavallaro, Gerald Jorge Lee, Charles Entrekin, Michael Theriault, Luke Wallin, James Dietrichson, Robert Frazier.

Cover and Artwork: Joseph Slusky

A SIMPLE INSTRUMENT: REMEMBERING THE BERKELEY POETS COOPERATIVE

Carter McKenzie

I have before me an image of a typewriter in flames. This postcard depicting Leopoldo M. Maler's piece, "Hommage," shows the force of what appears to be a simple instrument: rather than scrolling paper, the Underwood Standard Typewriter is emitting sheets of fire. I have kept the card on the shelf above my desk since it was given to me by a poet-friend six years ago on the occasion of her fortieth birthday— for me, the gesture was an affirmation of a shared commitment to the solitary work of creating art through language, despite the risks.

I did not know then that this art piece, included in the Hess Collection in Napa, California, has special personal significance for Maler, whose uncle is believed to have been killed as a result of his inflammatory political essays. Even without knowing this context, however, what remains fundamentally evocative in the image, offered by a fellow poet, is the association between fire and the demands of writing. My friend's sharing a copy of "Hommage" with each of the members of our Oregon poetry group was a way of acknowledging the necessity of continuing a singular path that we each fully recognized as our own.

I return to Maler's image now as an affirmation of shared resolve among poets as I remember being introduced to the Berkeley Poets Cooperative over twenty years ago. I had just moved to the Bay Area with my then-husband from Brooklyn, where we had lived for three years. During the time in New York I had begun to focus on the craft of poetry by seeking out exchanges with others, in addition to solitary practice. I was learning to bring poems out into the light, learning how to make them stronger, and learning how to know when to relentlessly start all over again. I was particularly fortunate to take part in a workshop with Joan Larkin at the Writer's Voice. Once in Berkeley, I received my first acceptances from the journals *Poets On:* and *Camellia.*

I recall sitting at a small, round-topped table next to the kitchen window in our rental house in El Cerrito one late summer morning, looking through the pages of *Poetry Flash,* which I had discovered at one of the bookstores I had come to appreciate in the Berkeley area—perhaps Black Oak Books or Pegasus—and seeing a notice inviting participants to the Berkeley Poets Cooperative. What was new for me was the invitation to a private home extended to anyone interested in participating in the critique group. My previous experience involved only workshops in public spaces. Other gatherings were by invitation only. Here there was no requirement to submit work beforehand; there was no screening. The ad simply communicated an invitation to anyone interested in writing poetry to join.

Poetry itself involves shifting and transforming boundaries of the public and private worlds; it makes possible through accomplished form a vital engagement of recognition and discovery. It reaches beyond the personality of the writer to the personal involvement of the reader in the life of language—a language that surprises us into new ways of connection. So I felt, as I attended each workshop in Gail and Charles's living room. Their willingness to keep the invitation open seemed like a realization of responsiveness to the possibilities of new connections. I attended the workshop as regularly as I could for at least two years because I was finally experiencing, primarily as a listener, sustained discussions of poetry, rather than simply individual responses to individual poems. And in terms of critique, I learned by attending this workshop a greater resilience and receptivity regarding criticism; I recognized this attendance as an opportunity of artistic challenge rather than easy reassurance.

Walking through Gail and Charles's door, I was aware of a family—a young child's drawing of a yellow sun on the wall next to the staircase; Charles sitting at the kitchen table finishing a bowl of soup before the workshop started; a teenage son sitting on the armrest of a sofa, quietly listening to poets read their work once the session had begun, before heading out with his own friends. I clearly remember the presence of Charles's son Demian, a poet who was present at every session I attended. I remember glimpses of the contexts of poems, such as a tour of the addition of a third floor to Gail and Charles's house one night, the subject of Gail's poem about the intensity of the lack of privacy during construction, which she may have read earlier that evening. As we admired the finished room overlooking trees, Gail momentarily curled up on a blue cushion in bliss. I did not know Gail well, but because I knew her poem I appreciated and remembered her gesture.

I shared with the group my first sonnet; I shared with them news of my pregnancy with my first child. In response to hearing about the pregnancy, one of the poets at the session remarked that becoming a parent is a humbling experience. I remember the comment as being a surprise, but also an insight regarding the creation process in general. Our work involves engagement with a force, within and beyond us, that will always be greater in its demands than we had imagined. At this workshop, compliments on poems brought in were not the point. Criticism was respectful, but specific, and most often helpful. This gathering, with its faith in the idea of keeping the door open, was about work and artistic growth—about putting the poems through a kind of fire. My connection with Berkeley Poets Cooperative existed because of the shared commitment to the craft of poetry, and it became memorable because of the personal associations made vivid through that artistic exchange.

I am grateful for the inclusion Gail and Charles offered, not only to friends and colleagues, but also to perfect strangers determined to develop their poetry. I am grateful for the authentic engagement during those workshop evenings in their living room in Berkeley, and for the existence of the rare cooperative spirit that made such an exchange possible. To this day, the fire connects us.

BERKELEY POETS COOPERATIVE/27

1986

Kim Addonizio, Bruce Hawkins, Rod Tulloss, Eliot Schain, Gerald Jorge Lee, Elizabeth Socolow, Carla Kandinsky, Bruce Boston, Linda Moyer, Jerry Ratch, Linda McFerrin, Jeffrey Zable, Tim Andersen, Jose F. Padua, Loss Pequeno Glazier, Mark Taksa, Linda Freymiller, Grace Grafton, Gail Rudd, J.D. Woolery, Mark Ray, John T. Selawsky, Marybeth Faldenstine, Susan M. Cosens, Philip Brady, Charles Entrekin, Alicia Ostriker, Jose Sequeira, Merle Bachman, Ivan Arguelles, Julia Vinograd, George W. Smythe, Candida Lawrence

Cover: Anthony Dubovsky
Artwork: Robert Brokl, Gary Sinick

POETRY FARM

Demian Entrekin

If you grew up on a farm, odds are pretty good that you know some things about farming. Your sense of the seasons and the weather are perhaps keener than most. If you grew up with parents who were attorneys, odds are pretty good you have a good feel for making your case. Of course, there's no guarantee in either case that you'll turn out to be a farmer (or lawyer).

I grew up in a house where people worked at poetry. People came together in our house on a regular basis to read, comment, argue, and sometimes even fight, about the craft of poetry. My father, Charles Entrekin, was the poet-in-chief of the house, and he was deeply involved in creating volumes of poetry and short fiction in a magazine known as the Berkeley Poets Workshop & Press. He also worked in the business world, but the business world was always "out there." It was poetry that was "in here." My stepmother, Maggie Entrekin Roizen, was the resident painter, and she was also actively involved in the craft of making poetry books.

There was a long and rugged cast of characters that came and went at our house. In Berkeley in the seventies, the world looked very different than it looks today. It was more freeform, more open-ended, more revolutionary. Anything could happen and often did. I remember late one night, after I had gone to bed, some raging writer coming to the door, screaming and beating himself on the head with his own shoe. Looking back now, I wonder if he was despairing because he just couldn't pull the poetry out of his head the way he needed to. When I went to Telegraph Avenue, I would nearly always run into Bruce Hawkins selling copies of the magazines made in my house.

Growing up, I moved in a different direction. There was no burning reason to go my own way, or at least not that I can remember. I was looking for a positive path of any kind. And so I fancied myself a mathematician and was attracted to that branch of philosophy where there was one correct answer and oceans of wrong answers. Math seemed like a place where I could pitch my own tent. One could do the work, derive the equations, and get to the results. QED. And I was able to get there often enough to see evidence of getting things right with regularity.

It's easy to see now that I had little idea what I was pursuing, and that I had even less of an idea of where it would take me. Somewhere during my time at UCLA, I discovered poetry and language. But of course I wasn't actually discovering poetry. I was remembering poetry. I was remembering language. I had grown up on the poetry farm, and it was a familiar place to do my work. After three years, my blue-collar math career ended before it started.

These days, I write mostly short fiction, and from time to time I will churn out an essay or a blog entry. I still wonder at times if I would have become a lover of language if I had grown up on a farm, and I will never know. But I do know that in the homes where I grew up, writing and language were always in the air and in the walls and in the furniture. At my house, you could smell the words (not to mention the turpentine).

Today I went back, dug around and found the last poem I wrote, which is right about the time when I started to write stories instead of poems on a regular basis. I guess I saw the change coming:

SMOKE (JULY 11, 2008)

Wanting to put them down
for a while, for just a little while,
all the phrases tumbling around
and around on the inside
of your head, your feverish head,
your combustible eloquence.

Wanting to silence the stream
of articulations, the florid
swirl of vernacular
the echoes of selfsame
counterpoint, the very words themselves.

Wanting to have the moment,
the yet unopened moment
of release, the loosening of time,
untangling of the needs,
the exhale of argument
in favor of something else entirely,
in favor of sight, perhaps
of color and temperature, of smell

the smell of sugar pine
or bay leaf, or even smoke,
yes smoke from wildfire,
an all consuming wildfire
to burn it all down,
so we can start over again.

BERKELEY POETS COOPERATIVE/28

1986

Contributors: Jerry Roscoe, Philip Brady, Robert Frazier, James Russell Williams, Jane Rice, Chitra Divakaruni, Steffen Horstmann, Carla Kandinsky, Bruce Hawkins, Marilee Richards, Mark Taksa, Linda Lancione Moyer, Thomas Wiloch, William Derge, John Selawsky, Loss Pequeño Glazier, Deborah Fruchey, Frances McCue, Linda Freymiller, Judy Cantera, Louis Phillips, Tobey Kaplan, Gail Rudd, Randall Potts, Gerald Lee, Charles Entrekin, Linda McFerrin, James Woolery, Albert Huffstickler, Susan Robertson, Michael Theriault

Cover: Anthony Dubovsky
Artwork: Sarah Bade

BPC Years: 1984–1988

THEY MADE A TABLE

Linda Lancione (formerly Moyer)

I thought I'd go to New York to become a novelist—I was majoring in literature at Cal and had taken a couple of creative writing courses; wasn't that what writers did, go to New York? Instead, I graduated one Saturday and was married the next. That was June 1963, the year before the Free Speech Movement. Nine years later—with two kids, two graduate degrees, and a store of experience working and traveling in Eastern Europe—my husband and I returned to a Berkeley full of foment.

Quickly caught up in the fevered politics of Berkeley feminism, I volunteered in a tiny, well-stocked feminist bookstore on Haste Street just off Telegraph called "Up Haste." I devoured the roster of contemporary women poets—Sylvia Plath, Anne Sexton, Robin Morgan, the lot—as well as forgotten or underrated women novelists and feminist tracts. Spurred, like so many women then, by the heady notion that my own experience and take on the world were fit subjects, I gradually reasserted my claim on writing.

In 1976 our family moved to Amsterdam, where I worked on poetry and fiction, out of which came a letterpress book of poems, handset by friends. I finished a novel. In 1980, back in Berkeley once more and teaching part-time, I pored over stapled-together chapbooks on the local poets' shelf at Cody's. Among them were Alta, whose Shameless Hussy Press published Susan Griffin and Ntosake Shange, as well as her own poems, and John Oliver Simon, publisher of *Aldebaran Review* and his own work, who could be seen bravely patrolling Telegraph Avenue, peddling his books. (Little did I know that I would one day share a grandchild with John Oliver Simon and Alta.) I wondered: Was I a poet? Did I qualify? Longing for a community of writers, I hung out at readings, smiling shyly at hip-looking, confident strangers who gazed right through me. Eventually, I found my way through a listing in *Poetry Flash* to the Berkeley Poets Co-op.

They made a table and I sat down. It was exhilarating to walk the few blocks from our house south of campus to the Entrekins', haul copies of my poems out of my bag, and begin. Everyone had a day job they didn't complain about. I knew much less than I thought I did but eventually concluded that was also true of almost everyone else in the room. Still, for the duration of the evening, we apprenticed ourselves to each other. Nobody raved over my poems, but occasionally someone would say, "nice sounds here" or "lovely image there." As I heard Grace Paley say once, "You can live a long time on a little nice." Charles always wanted to cut my last lines. "Here's where this poem ends, Linda." To this day I put my poems through that Entrekin filter. Some memories are indelible: Chitra Divakaruni reading her lush poems in lovely, India-inflected English, Marilee Richards' profound and deeply witty cow poems, the guy next to me on the couch who kept surreptitiously trying to stroke my hand. I'd go home full of excitement; words and phrases hummed in my head all night. Every Wednesday, I had a place to go where poetry was spoken.

Over the several years I was part of the Co-op, I had my moments of discontent. I sometimes trudged home from the workshop grumbling to myself about people who insisted on writing poems bereft of punctuation, for example, or poems that rhymed too insistently. More seriously, I questioned how much I'd come to tamp down my own weirdness, or wildness, in order to win the group's approval. I often felt tension between the need for feedback and stimulation from a community of poets and the inner longing just to close the door and write from the deep self.

But the past keeps changing, as the title of poet Chana Bloch's book instructs us. With distance, the fact that such a loose-knit, shape-shifting assembly of poets met at all, and for so many years, is a wonder. It amazes me even more how a group open to everyone self-selected for seriousness. It's remarkable, too, how many of us have kept at the work of writing, some with high name recognition, most with less. I value the Co-op now for other qualities I then took for granted: its camaraderie, its independence from institutions, the opportunity to play an editorial role on our high-quality quarterly journal. (Whenever a publication is slow getting back to me, I picture the poetry editors of issue #29—Mark Taksa, Marilee Richards, Bruce Hawkins and me—sitting around a kitchen table bleary-eyed, plowing through hundreds of folded batches of submissions disgorged from brown-paper grocery bags). None of this would have been possible without the inspiration, devotion, and hospitality of Charles Entrekin and Gail Rudd.

BERKELEY POETS COOPERATIVE/29

1987

Contributors: Martha Elizabeth, Charles Entrekin, Ursula K. LeGuin, Tony D'Arpino, Susan Herron Sibbet, Roque Dalton, Bonnie Auslander, Rane Arroyo, Cole Swensen, Walter McDonald, James Sutherland-Smith, Linda Lancione Moyer, John Smith, Mark Taksa, Robert Frazier, Bruce Boston, Bruce Hawkins, Frances Spickerman, Judy Clarence, Richard Hoebel, Carla Kandinsky, Julia Vinograd, Joanna Warwick, Jean Vengua Gier, Chitra Divakaruni, Jane Rice, William C. Schillaci, Sena Jeter Naslund, Gordon Carrega, Stephen-Paul Martin, Luke Wallin

Cover: Anthony Dubovsky
Artwork: Anne Hawkins

SOME THOUGHTS ABOUT THE BERKELEY POETS CO-OP

Chitra Divakaruni

I clearly remember the first time I attended a Berkeley Poets Co-op workshop. I remember standing outside Gail and Charles Entrekin's tree-shaded house in Berkeley in a darkening evening in 1985, holding on to the slip of paper with their address, my heart hammering. I had recently graduated from UC Berkeley with a degree in literature. I knew a lot about literary criticism, but in terms of my own creative work, I was a fledgling writer, and this was my first workshop, apart from a very academic one I'd taken in college. I was so nervous I could barely read out the poem I'd brought, or make sense of the comments that were offered afterward by workshop members. I do remember that people were positive and encouraging. Gail and Charles always made sure that while members gave honest criticism, they were never unkind, and that did a lot to boost my confidence.

Being a member of the workshop was very helpful to me. I was the only writer of Indian origin in the group, and the comments gave me a good sense of what people unfamiliar with my culture could understand of my work, what they were able to relate to. It gave me a lasting belief that good literature, while it is precise and authentic in its details, is also universal. That is something I've striven towards ever since.

Berkeley Poets Co-op provided me with a writing community, something that is very empowering for new (and continuing) writers. At that time, I lived in a suburban world down south in Fremont, among people who, though well-meaning, were mystified by my desire to be a writer. It was wonderful to come to the workshop and be around people who completely understood the burning urge to create a world out of words. One of my first poems to be published, called "Each Night," was accepted for publication by the Berkeley Poets Co-op Magazine. That was an amazing moment.

EACH NIGHT

After it is over
his breath thickens into sleep.
Pinned under his damp arm
she closes dry eyes.

And stands on the bridge
watching the water,
brackish brown
laden with anemones.

Feels the whirr of gnats
against their petals, against
her hand. Her fingers reach
for the largest anemone
tipping out the water.

Sliding into the stream
she swells like a rotting branch
and watches the thickening green
close over her head.

Her eyes are pebbles, smooth and slippery
in stagnant water.
Somewhere a submarine light
distends the underneath of an anemone
which floats huge and purple
over her spreading hair
suspended in a shadow
that is calm
and circular.

The Co-op also published my book of poetry, *The Reason for Nasturtiums*. I still remember the disbelieving joy when I held that slim volume in my hands.

Now, as a writer and teacher of writing in the Creative Writing program at the University of Houston, I strongly recommend to writers who are on their own to look for a good writing group in their community that they can join. A good writing group gives you feedback that helps you see your work in a different light, keeps you writing (because now there's pressure to present to your group at regular times), and supports you through your writing successes and disappointments. Berkeley Poets Co-op certainly did all that for me—and I am forever grateful.

BERKELEY POETS COOPERATIVE/30

1989

Contributors: Randall Watson, Jay Griswold, Rod Tulloss, Belden Johnson, Marilee Richards, James Woolery, Chitra Divakaruni, James Russell Williams, Laura Conway, Demian Entrekin, Jane Rice, James Sutherland-Smith, Robert Dilallo, Patricia Dienstfrey, Alicia Ostriker, Bruce Hawkins, Charles Entrekin, Lucille Day, Betsy Dubovsky, Carla Kandinsky, Robert Frazier, Charles London Cyndian, Mark Taksa, Luis Phillips, Gail Rudd Entrekin, Linda Watanabe McFerrin, Linda Lancione Moyer, Bruce Boston, Arthur Dembling

Cover: Anthony Dubovsky
Artwork: Steven Raskin

BPC Years: 1984-1990

ONE DOOR CLOSES

Linda Watanabe McFerrin

Put me last.

Call it the caboose—the final car in a train that you don't want to miss. Maybe you've run just fast enough to catch up with it and hop aboard as the train pulls out of the station. You grab the end ladder, the one behind the back wheels, and then you are on it … but just barely. It was like that when I joined the Berkeley Poets Cooperative. I was on that last car. I'd missed the wild and crazy sixties, the seventies, what I thought must have been the cool, Telegraph Avenue street-poetry days. They were history. The year was 1984, and I'm well aware of how fortunate I was to catch the tail end of the Co-op's incredible ride.

Did I mention that I was a zombie at the time? Well, at least that is when I began writing about zombies. I was wandering through the post-apocalyptic ruin of my still-young life, having lost my newborn daughter. She died in my arms in hospital. I was living in the East Bay, in Oakland, after dropping out—first from the fashion industry, then from the art world—to start a family. Cruel joke, and the last time I tried that. The only thing standing between the absolute end and me was some volunteer work I was doing for The Hunger Project and a blank book that my husband had wisely given me. I had writers in my family. My grandfather was a Welsh journalist in pre-war Shanghai. My aunt was a screenwriter. One of my uncles was an American war correspondent, and my mother would have liked to be a poet or maybe a novelist … if she hadn't had her hands full with the four children, whom she seemed to like a lot more than her writing. I was encouraged to write, and I loved doing it, but only for school or for pleasure.

In 1984, it had become something more than that. The pages of that blank book would become an empty wasteland I would first puzzle over, then use as the space to create a map back. I'm not sure what provoked me to call up the people who organized the Berkeley Poets Cooperative. I'm certain my hand shook as I dialed the number.

"Hello?"

"Hi, this is Gail."

"Is this the Berkeley Poets Co-op? I was thinking of ..."

"Yes, come on over. We'd love it if you joined us."

Gail.

Does she know that I will always love her for that?

Not everyone was as welcoming as Gail. It didn't matter. Gail is generous and generative enough to mother a huge tribe. She and Charles, the Co-op founder, lived together, and although they weren't married at the time, it was immediately clear that these two were very much in love. That love permeated their poems and filled the space around them. To me, tottering as I was on the verge of disintegration, it was manna. They made it a comforting and colorful space, as did Carla Kandinsky and Jamie Woolery and Gerry Lee and Elise Morgan and Chitra Divakaruni, too, when she briefly joined the group.

Every week, I would bring some horrid little poem to the meeting and the other poets would chop it to bits. I liked that. It suited my frame of mind. I learned to ignore the less-than-pleasant people in the room, and I did overcome my fear of the Bruces—Hawkins and Boston— longtime members whom I found both brilliant and intimidating.

FIREFLIES AFTER THUNDER . . .
for Lowry

Fireflies after thunder:
lights winking on as if
life scattered kisses — dandelion-light —
into the dark cloud damp,
and they have stuck there
on a fly-paper of shadow,
on a moment that, like a shade drawn,
counts itself down.
And the moisture rises up,
a hand's heel pressing into my cranium.
Fireflies follow, their flickering lights —
Hatchlings, a contagion — touch of life and death
that I now carry inside me.

I can see why the Co-op thrived for all those years. In general the sessions were thrilling—full of risk and dread and elation. Charles and Gail were the perfect hosts. Charles is a fantastic editor. Any of us could volunteer to work with him on the BPW&P anthologies, which I did. I sometimes think of that first experience after all these years of editing books. Charles is a genius. Everyone was opinionated. Not a lesson was wasted. I still don't understand why more people didn't seize the opportunity to work with Charles on those projects.

By the time Charles and Gail moved the Co-op to Dana Street, I'd decided to pursue a graduate degree in creative writing at San Francisco State University, so I started studying language poetry with Barrett Watten, contemporary women's poetry with Kathleen Fraser, and memoir with Michael Rubin. Anne Rice's husband, Stan Rice, was department chair at the time. Stan was a poet and artist, though I also took a short story class with him. Anne's novel, *Interview with the Vampire*, had been published nearly a decade before. For my oral exams at the end of the program, I chose John Ashbery, whom I interviewed; William Shakespeare, whom I could not interview; and Yukio Mishima, whose work Michael read and studied just so that he could serve as my examiner. I did well. I earned the degree. Not long afterward Michael died, and I realized how sick he had been when he tackled Mishima—a complex, darkly driven writer—for me.

In 1990, the Berkeley Poets Workshop and Press published two chapbooks: *The Reason for Nasturtiums* by Chitra Banerjee Divakaruni and my first book, *The Impossibility of Redemption Is Something We Hadn't Figured On*—the last to come out from the Co-op before Gail and Charles moved north to Nevada City. I switched shortly thereafter to prose, both fiction and nonfiction. I wrote for newspapers and magazines for years. *Namako: Sea Cucumber*, *The Hand of Buddha*, and *Dead Love*—my ultimate zombie exorcism—are among my book-length titles. I'm still in touch with my favorite Co-op members. Bruce Boston turned out to be something of a mentor. I have him to thank for the direction that lead me to place as a finalist for a Bram Stoker Award. Every so often—not often enough, though—I see Charles and Gail, and I've been delighted to have them as speakers and members of my own writers' organization, Left Coast Writers®, now in its seventh year.

It turns out that the last car of the train is as good as any on a trip like this one. I tell that to all my students these days. Last car or first, take a chance. Run for it. Jump aboard. The journey regretted is always the one not taken.

FREIGHT TRAIN

The freight train moans toward the docks
just as I cry, working my way into my metal future.

There is no door in the bright sky
from which God descends on a cloud of steam.

But there is an ocean close by.
It creaks with ships.

On my black track, I clatter toward oblivion,
find solace in the vast wings of the albatross.

Contributors:

RAMSAY BELL BRESLIN, M.A., M.F.A., is a poet, art writer, editor, and publisher (Kelsey Street Press). Her reviews have appeared in *Threepenny Review* and the *East Bay Express* and her poems are published in *Blink* and *Slurve*. She is at work on a biography of Bay Area sculptor Stephen De Staebler. Her essay on mourning in De Staebler's works (*fort da* psychoanalytic journal) will appear in a collection of psycho-biographical essays, *Examining Lives: Seeking Others, Finding Ourselves* (Oxford University Press). In 2012, Ramsay conceived and curated *The Reading Room*, the Berkeley Art Museum's tribute to the history of East Bay literary publishing.

BRUCE BOSTON is the author of more than fifty books and chapbooks. His writing has appeared in *Asimov's SF, Amazing Stories, Weird Tales, Strange Horizons, Year's Best Fantasy and Horror*, and *The Nebula Awards Showcase*. Boston has won the Bram Stoker Award for Poetry, the *Asimov's* Readers Award, and the Rhysling Award, each a record number of times. He has also received a Pushcart Prize for fiction and the Grandmaster Award of the Science Fiction Poetry Association. He will be Poet Guest of Honor at the 2013 Bram Stoker Awards/World Horror Con to be held in New Orleans. www.bruceboston.com

MICHAEL COVINO is the author of three books: a poetry collection *Unfree Associations*, a short story collection, *The Off-Season*, and a novel, *The Negative*.

LUCILLE LANG DAY is the author of a memoir, *Married at Fourteen* (Heyday, 2012). She has also published a children's book (*Chain Letter,* 2005) and eight poetry collections and chapbooks, most recently *The Curvature of Blue* (Cervena Barva, 2009). Her poetry and prose have appeared widely in such magazines and anthologies as *The Cincinnati Review, The Hudson Review,* and *New Poets of the American West* (Many Voices, 2010). She received her M.A. in English and M.F.A. in Creative Writing at San Francisco State University, and her M.A. in Zoology and Ph.D. in Science and Mathematics Education at the University of California at Berkeley. http://lucillelangday.com.

PATRICIA DIENSTFREY'S publications include *The Woman Without Experiences* (Kelsey Street, 1995), winner of the America Award for Fiction; *Love and Illustration* (a+bend press, 2000); and *The Grand Permission: New Writings on Poetics and Motherhood* (Wesleyan, 2003, co-edited with Brenda Hillman.) Her work has appeared in anthologies, including *Moving Borders: Three Decades of Innovative Writing by Women* (Talisman House, 1997, editor: Mary Margaret Sloan) and *The Addison Street Anthology: Berkeley's Poetry Walk* (Heyday Books, 2004, editors: Robert Hass and Jessica Fisher.) She is a co-founder of Kelsey Street Press, established in 1974 to publish innovative writing by women.
www.kelseyst.com

CHITRA BANERJEE DIVAKARUNI is an award-winning author, poet, and teacher. Her themes include women, immigration, the South Asian experience, history, myth, magical realism, and diversity. She writes for adults and children. Her books have been translated into 29 languages, including Dutch, Hebrew, Russian, and Japanese. Two novels, *The Mistress of Spices* and *Sister of My Heart*, have been made into films. Her short story collection, *Arranged Marriage*, won an American Book Award. She teaches Creative Writing at the University of Houston.
www.chitradivakaruni.com

CHARLES ENTREKIN'S most recently published works include a novel, *Red Mountain, Birmingham, Alabama, 1965* (El Leon Literary Arts, 2008), and *Listening: New and Selected Works* (Poetic Matrix Press, 2010) and he is the author of four books of poems and stories. Charles was a founder and managing editor of *The Berkeley Poets Cooperative* and *The Berkeley Poets Workshop & Press,* and was a co-founder/advisory board member of Literature Alive!, a nonprofit organization in Nevada County, California. He is co-editor of the e-zine *Sisyphus,* a magazine of literature, philosophy, and culture, and managing editor of Hip Pocket Press. Charles is the father of five children and lives in the San Francisco Bay Area with his wife, poet Gail Rudd Entrekin.
(www.charlesentrekin.com)
(www.hippocketpress.com)

DEMIAN ENTREKIN is an early-stage technology entrepreneur in the San Francisco Bay Area and has founded two successful software companies. He holds an M.A. in English from San Francisco State University and has published poems, stories, and articles in journals and small press magazines. He authors an award-winning technology blog called Future States (published by IT Toolbox) and has published numerous papers on software development and the software industry. He is also a regular contributor on Vator.tv, a web site that covers entrepreneurial business and industry trends.

GAIL RUDD ENTREKIN is editor of the online environmental literary journal *Canary* and Poetry Editor of Hip Pocket Press. She has taught English Literature and Creative Writing in California colleges for over 25 years and has published four books of poetry, the most recent being *Rearrangement of the Invisible* (Poetic Matrix Press, 2012). Her poems have been widely published in anthologies and journals, including *Cimarron Review, Nimrod, The Ohio Journal*, and *Southern Poetry Review*, and were finalists for the Pablo Neruda Prize from *Nimrod* in 2011.
www.hippocketpress.org/canary.cfm

MARCIA FALK's poetry books are *This Year in Jerusalem, It Is July in Virginia*, and *My Son Likes Weather*. She is also the author of *The Book of Blessings* (a bilingual re-creation of Jewish prayer in poetic forms) and several books of translation from Hebrew and Yiddish, including *The Song of Songs, The Spectacular Difference: Selected Poems of Zelda*, and *With Teeth in the Earth: Selected Poems of Malka Heifetz Tussman*. She received a Ph.D. from Stanford and was a professor of literature and creative writing for many years. Her words have been set to music by over thirty composers. She also paints; view her art at marciafalk.com.

TED FLEISCHMAN was born in Chicago. Graduate of University of Chicago. MS Physics. Secular Jew. Sometimes distracted. Always interested in discovering the underlying mechanisms that shape our existence.

STEWART FLORSHEIM was the editor of *Ghosts of the Holocaust* (Wayne State University Press, 1989), an anthology of poetry by children of Holocaust survivors. He wrote the poetry chapbook, *The Girl Eating Oysters* (2River, 2004). Stewart won the Blue Light Book Award for *The Short Fall From Grace* (Blue Light Press, 2006). His most recent collection, *A Split Second of Light* (Blue Light Press, 2011), received an Honorable Mention in the San Francisco Book Festival. He has been awarded residencies from Artcroft and the Kimmel Harding Nelson Center for the Arts. Stewart has held readings in the Bay Area, New York, Boston, London, and Jerusalem.
www.stewartflorsheim.com

ANNE AND BRUCE HAWKINS enjoy their privacy.

MICHAEL HELM has written about and helped celebrate Northern California's alternative culture for forty-three years (1969-2012). He is the editor/publisher of *City Miner* magazine and City Miner Books and the author of two books of poetry, *The Familiar Stranger* and *Snap Thoughts*. His poetry and short fiction have appeared in *Ball, Fiction, North Country Star, Green Revolution, Voices International* and the *Berkeley Poets Cooperative Magazine*. Mr. Helm has contributed numerous interviews, feature articles and book reviews to *City Miner, East Bay Express* and *San Francisco Chronicle* and is the author of three books about thoroughbred horse-racing, including the critically praised *A Breed Apart*. Mike Helm has lived in Fort Bragg, California, since 2002.
cminer@mcn.org

B. NINA HOLZER grew up in the Austrian Alps and came to the United States as a college student. She attended San Francisco State University, University of California at San Diego, and Sonoma State University, receiving graduate degrees in Literature, Creative Writing, and Psychology. As a bilingual writer and teacher whose mother tongue is German, her primary language is English. A student of Native American languages, she lived with Native people for large parts of her life. Holzer publishes poetry, prose, literary translations, journals, articles on the creative process, and body-mind health. She lives near the Klamath River in Northern California, creating Art, Gardens, Good Food, Rituals to Heal, and always loves to tell a story.

BELDEN JOHNSON published *Snake Blossoms* (1976) with the Berkeley Poets Workshop & Press, and has since published a novel, *Fathers and Teachers* (2008) and the nonfiction *Real Relationship: Essential Tools to Help You Go the Distance* (2012), both with CreateSpace, a subsidiary of Amazon. He moved into the forest outside Nevada City in 1982 where he lives and works with his wife, Dr. Yashi Amita Johnson, at The Center for Inner Vision. They share a meadow with a bobcat, a family of bears, a golden eagle, and a multitude of birds. Belden has, so far, two grandchildren.
www.centerforinnervisions.com

CARLA KANDINSKY published in BPC and subsequently participated in the 1999 Summer Institute of Literature of Northern California at UC Davis, featured in the Literature of Northern California section with such well-known authors as Jane Hirschfield and Malcolm Margolin. Carla received a Certificate of Completion in both Fiction Writing and Poetry from Berkeley City College; worked on the staff of *Milvia Street*, BCC's literary journal; published in several issues of the magazine; and teaches the Summer Writing Intensive. She teaches a memoir class at the North Berkeley Senior Center. Kandinsky is published in over fifty small press magazines and anthologies.

TOBEY KAPLAN is a poet who teaches Literature, Composition, and Humanities in the San Francisco Bay Area at Chabot, Laney, and Merritt Colleges. She is an active member of California Poets in the Schools, giving readings, workshops, and presentations throughout the country regarding creative process, literacy, and social change. She is a Dorland Mountain Colony Fellow, an Affiliate Artist at the Headlands Center for the Arts, and was a recipient of a New Langton Arts Award in 1996. She is author of *Across the Great Divide* (Androgyne, 1995). She mentors Native American adults and children, advocating cultural empowerment through creative process with imaginative language.

MARILYN KING did her graduate work in creative writing at San Francisco State University. With a background in advertising copywriting and college English tutoring, she still considers herself a beginner at poetry. Her work has appeared in the *Marin Poetry Center Anthology*, *Poetry Farmers Almanac*, *Berkeley Poets Cooperative*, and *Whistlestop Express*.

CHARLES KLEIN worked as an early childhood educator, teacher, director, and college instructor. Klein exhibits his photographs throughout the United States. His images and designs have appeared in over 80 book jackets worldwide, for authors including E.L. Doctorow, Paul Auster, Charles Baxter, Sena Jeter Naslund, Ivan Klima, and Andrew Solomon. A new photo essay on the 2003 anti-Iraq war protest in San Francisco will appear in Spring 2013 in *Mount Hope* literary magazine. Throughout his career, Klein composed poems and songs, recently collaborating with Albanian soul rapper Jemayli. He raised six children and lives happily in Berkeley with his third wife.

http://www.charleskleinphotography.com/

NAOMI RUTH LOWINSKY lives at the confluence of the River Psyche and the Deep River of poetry. Her recent memoir, *The Sister from Below: When the Muse Gets Her Way* tells stories of her pushy muse. She is the co-editor, with Patricia Damery, of the new collection *Marked by Fire: Stories of the Jungian Way*. She is also the author of four books of poetry, including *The Faust Woman Poems* (forthcoming). She is a member analyst of the San Francisco Jung Institute and has for years led a writing circle there called Deep River.

www.sisterfrombelow.com

CLIVE MATSON (M.F.A. Columbia University) was drafted as *Chalcedony's* (kal-SAID-'n-ease) astonished scribe in 2004. His early teachers were Beats in New York City, and, amazingly, his seventh book was placed in John Wieners' coffin. He became immersed in the stream of passionate intensity that runs through us all and has finally stopped trying to go anywhere else. He writes from the itch in his body, to the delight of his students, and that's old hat, according to *Let the Crazy Child Write!* (1998), the text he uses to make his living, teaching creative writing. The City of Berkeley awarded Clive a Lifetime Achievement Award in 2012. He enjoys playing basketball, table tennis, and collecting minerals in the field. He lives in Oakland, California, where he helps bring up his teenage son, Ezra.

www.matsonpoet.com

LINDA WATANABE MCFERRIN has been traveling since she was two and writing about it since she was six. A poet, travel writer, and novelist, she is the author of two poetry collections; an award-winning novel *Namako: Sea Cucumber* (Coffee House Press); and the short story collection *The Hand of Buddha* (Coffee House Press). She is the editor of a travel guidebook *Best Places Northern California, 4th ed.* and four literary anthologies. A past winner of the *Nimrod* International Katherine Anne Porter Prize for Fiction, she teaches and leads workshops in fiction and creative non-fiction. Her novel, *Dead Love* (Stonebridge Press, 2010), is a Bram Stoker Award finalist for Superior Achievement in a Novel and current candidate for a Carl Brandon Society Award.
www.lwmcferrin.com
www.deadlovebook.com

CARTER MCKENZIE'S poems have appeared in a number of journals and anthologies, including *What the River Brings: Oregon River Poems* (editor: Kathryn Ridall). She is the author of *Naming Departure*, a chapbook of poetry published by Traprock Books in 2004. Her full-length book of poetry *Out of Refusal*, published by Airlie Press, was released to bookstores in October, 2010. In addition to teaching, editing, and writing, Carter studies and performs songs in the Scottish Gaelic language with the women's a cappella group Kitchen Ceilidh.

LINDA LANCIONE MOYER'S varied writing life has included publication of two travel guides; three poetry chapbooks; and publication of poems or personal essays in a number of journals, most recently *Connecticut Review, The Pearl, Harpur Palate, The Pinch* and *New Letters*. Her *New Letters* essay, "The Currency of Love," won the 2010 essay contest and was nominated for a Pushcart Prize. Among other residencies, Linda received a fellowship at the Montalvo Arts Center for 2013.

PETER NAJARIAN received an NEA grant (2000) for his most recent book, *The Artist and His Mother* (Fresno University Press, 2010), a creative nonfiction novel. *The Great American Loneliness* (Blue Crane Books, 1998), an illustrated collection of fiction and non-fiction, featured "Storytime," originally published by the BPC. *Daughters of Memory* (City Miner, 1986, published by Mike Helm) was reviewed in the *New York Times Book Review*. The author created the illustrations and cover for that book and *Voyages* (Pantheon Books, 1971/Ararat Press,1980) and *Wash Me On Home, Mama,* (BPW&P, 1978). The cover art is sketched by the author and refined by artist/designer/Co-op member Tony Dubovsky and Dave Bullen of Northpoint Press.

ALICIA OSTRIKER 'S life changed when she joined BPC in 1973. She got a lot happier, she made friends who are still dear friends, she recognized that there are many different ways to write a poem, and she was inspired to co-found "US1 Poets-Co-op" in NJ, which still exists. BPC published her chapbook *A Dream of Springtime,* and she has since published eight volumes of poetry with the University of Pittsburgh Press—ncluding *The Mother/child Papers, The Imaginary Lover, The Crack in Everything,* and *The Book of Seventy,* as well as several books on poetry and on the Bible.
www.rci.rutgers.edu/~**ostriker**/home.htm

MARILEE RICHARDS, after writing her essay for *The Berkeley Poets Cooperative: A History of the Times*, re-discovered her poetic voice and began writing poems again. "One Explanation" appeared in the December 2012 issue of *Rattle.* She continues to introduce people to poetry via her spring and fall poetry-hiking classes, which are growing in size and popularity, and also leads a monthly writing workshop.

SUSAN STERN (director, producer, writer, narrator) has been a journalist specializing in investigative reporting for more than twenty years. Her articles have been published in the *Boston Globe, Sacramento Bee, San Francisco Examiner,* and *Oakland Tribune. The Wall Street Journal* credited Stern's expose of Navy base closures with, "saving thousands of local jobs." Stern has also written and produced news for KPIX TV, San Francisco's CBS affiliate. She is married to Spain, the cartoonist and artist. Their daughter, Nora, inspired her film, *Barbie Nation.* Stern's latest film, *The Self-Made Man,* was nominated for two Emmy Awards.
www.theselfmademan.com

MARK TAKSA'S most recent of ten chapbooks is *The Torah at the End of the Train* (Poetica Publishing Company, 2009), which received *Poetica Magazine's* annual chapbook award. Mark, along with Ted Fleischman, is currently the key coordinator of the long-standing Berkeley Poets Workshop. His affiliation with the BPC goes back to 1978. Now retired, Taksa and his wife Jan devote themselves to art and writing, to their family, and to their Jewish community as members of Oakland's First Hebrew Congregation, Temple Sinai, where he has been involved with writing liturgy for the Brotherhood Shabbat program and a poetry reading series.

ROD TULLOSS has been writing since his early teens. He received a B.S. in Mathematics and Philosophy from Union College (New York, 1966), an M.S. in Mathematics, and a PhD from the Group in Logic and the Methodology of Science (University of California at Berkeley, 1971). As a managing researcher in digital electronics, he achieved the honor of Fellow of Bell Laboratories. For the last 35 years, he has carried out taxonomic and systematic research on the mushroom family *Amanitaceae*. He established a nonprofit corporation, saving the majority of farmland in his current hometown from development, using the New Jersey Farmland Preservation program. He was a co-founder of both BPC and the US1 Writers Cooperative (Princeton, NJ). Unfortunately, he lost two decades of poetry writing to a series of medications that suppressed poetry entirely. He enjoys reading good writing aloud to any audience that will sit still for it.

DOROTHY WALL is author of *Identity Theory: New and Selected Poems, 1980-2010* (Blue Light Press, 2012) and *Encounters with the Invisible: Unseen Illness, Controversy, and Chronic Fatigue Syndrome* (Southern Methodist University Press, 2005), and coauthor of *Finding Your Writer's Voice: A Guide to Creative Fiction* (St. Martin's Press, 1994). Her poems, essays, and articles have appeared in numerous magazines and anthologies. She has taught Poetry and Fiction Writing at San Francisco State University, Napa Valley College, and UC Berkeley Extension, and since 1984 has run a writing consulting business in Berkeley.
www.dorothywall.com

Titles Published by BPW&P

Boston, Bruce - Jackbird
Boston, Bruce - She Comes When You're Leaving
Brodine, Karen - Slow Juggling
Coon, Betty - Seaward
Covino, Michael - Unfree Associations
Day, Lucille - Self-Portrait with Hand Microscope
Dienstfrey, Patricia - Newspaper Stories & Other Poems
Divakaruni, Chitra - The Reason for Nasturtiums
Entrekin, Charles - All Pieces of a Legacy
Entrekin, Charles - Casting for the Cutthroat & Other Poems
Entrekin, Charles - In This Hour
Entrekin, Gail Rudd - John Danced
Entrekin, Gail Rudd - You Notice the Body
Fleischman, Ted - Half a Bottle of Catsup
Frazier, Robert - Perception Barriers
Hawkins, Bruce - Wordrows
Hawkins, Bruce - The Ghost of the Buick
Johnson, Belden - Snake Blossoms
Kandinsky, Carla - Instead of a Camera
Lee, Gerald Jorge - Dancing at Ground Zero
McFerrin, Linda Watanabe - The Impossibility of Redemption Is Something
We Hadn't Figured On
Najarian, Peter - Wash Me On Home, Mama
Ostriker, Alicia - Once More Out of Darkness and other poems
Stone, Jennifer - Over by the Caves
Taksa, Mark - Truant Bather
Tulloss, Rod - The Machine Shuts Down
Woolery, J.D. - By Parked Cars

Photo: Stewart Florsheim

Members of the Berkeley Poets Cooperative
Morgan Hill, CA 1979

CPSIA information can be obtained at www.ICGtesting.com
Printed in the USA
BVOW10s1637250713

326906BV00007B/14/P